EQUIP LEADERS

Small Group Prison Ministry

EQUIP LEADERS

Small Group Prison Ministry

1 East Bode Road
Streamwood, IL 60107-6658 U.S.A.
awana.org
(630) 213-2000

© 2015 Awana® Clubs International

1   2   3   4   5   6   20   19   18   17   16   15

Table of Contents

CHAPTER 1
Ministry for Life Change 7

CHAPTER 2
Hand on the Word 27

CHAPTER 3
Hand on the Student 45

CHAPTER 4
Gospel of Grace 63

CHAPTER 5
Guide for Life Change 83

APPENDIX A
Gospel Wheel 108

APPENDIX B
Scripture Memory 111

BIBLIOGRAPHY 116

Chapter 1

REMEMBER THE PRISONER

*Remember those who are in prison,
as though in prison with them,
and those who are mistreated,
since you also are in the body.*

Hebrews 13:3

Memory Verses

KEY VERSE

Remember the Prisoner

Remember those who are in prison, as though in prison with them, and those who are mistreated, since you also are in the body. (Hebrews 13:3)

CHALLENGE VERSE 1

Praying for Prisoners

So Peter was kept in prison, but earnest prayer for him was made to God by the church. (Acts 12:5)

CHALLENGE VERSES 2

The Way of the Righteous

Blessed is the man who walks not in the counsel of the wicked, nor stands in the way of sinners, nor sits in the seat of scoffers; but his delight is in the law of the LORD, and on His law he meditates day and night. He is like a tree planted by streams of water that yields its fruit in its season, and its leaf does not wither. In all that he does, he prospers. The wicked are not so, but are like chaff that the wind drives away. Therefore the wicked will not stand in the judgment, nor sinners in the congregation of the righteous; for the LORD knows the way of the righteous, but the way of the wicked will perish. (Psalm 1)

CHAPTER 1

Ministry for Life Change

BIG IDEA

Prison ministry is service to the Lord by visiting, teaching, guiding, and advising those in prison to trust in Christ and to reach out to impact others, especially their children. **Why should I do this?** is the motivational question.

FOUNDATION

The biblical command in Hebrews 13:3 is not a suggestion. Remembering those who are in prison could be done from a distance. Prayer, support of chaplains, and providing literature are all significant aids in prison ministry. But if real life change is to happen, people have to be involving themselves in personal interaction. Visiting, praying with, facilitating small groups, and other intentional, consistent service all become the basis of our work in the prison. Not that prison ministry isn't hard, it is. The apostle Paul said that he worked, toiled, and struggled with all the energy that the Holy Spirit supplied (Colossians 1:29). Can we do any less for the incarcerated? Prison ministry expert Lennie Spitale highlights, "I do not know of any more fertile ground for the gospel in all of the United States than our jails and prisons. I make that statement unequivocally and without reservation."[1]

> Remembering those who are in prison

Art Rorheim, Co-founder of Awana®, challenged a group of inmates at the Louisiana State Penitentiary (also known as Angola) to memorize Psalm 1. Art regularly memorizes Scripture — a huge understatement considering this 95+-year-old leader! The psalm contrasts the way of the righteous with the way of the wicked. As the verses portray, a person who makes the Word of God his delight and meditation will prosper. Over a decade later the Psalm 1 Club among prisoners continues to have impact. In one of those first visits, Art recollects, "We were in one of the chapels, and I remember asking how many of the men there would be interested if there were something we could do to help their children. And all over the room, hands just shot up in the air. And it hasn't stopped there. I've continued to challenge these men to get into the Word and to memorize and learn Scripture because that is what we are all about here at Awana."[2]

The ministry that began with this kind of interaction has blossomed into Awana Lifeline™ prison ministries. Malachi Dads™ is the core program for male inmates, based upon the last verse in the Old Testament: *And he will turn the hearts of fathers to their children and the hearts of children to their fathers, lest I come and strike the land with a decree of utter destruction (Malachi 4:6).* Malachi Dads purposes to develop community and help men live up to their biblical responsibility as a dad. Hannah's Gift™ is the female inmate vehicle to help moms parent from a distance, just like Hannah in 1 Samuel. Returning Hearts Celebration™ seeks to unite inmates and their children for a day of games, food, relationship building, and Bible teaching. The stated vision of Awana Lifeline is "that every child would have a godly father and mother who are building a legacy of faith in Christ. To this end, our mission is to glorify God by inspiring and equipping men and women, families, churches, and communities to develop godly parents."[3]

Awana Lifeline –
building a legacy
of faith in Christ

PRINCIPLES

Definitions for This Ministry

Caring — Does visiting the incarcerated person or leading a prison Bible study qualify as ministry? Yes, but isn't ministry better understood as preaching to people? No, in fact, ministry in the New Testament has several of its prominent aspects "caring for those in prison (Matthew 25:44), serving tables (i.e., meeting physical needs) (Acts 6:2), and teaching the Word of God (Acts 6:4), giving money to meet others' needs (2 Corinthians 9:1), and all the service offered by Christians to others to build them up in faith."[4] Preaching may be an avenue of teaching the Word, but within the small-group prison ministry it cannot be the focus. (More about this in Chapter 5.) The concentration must be that of caring.

Teaching — What is the ministry of teaching? We will use this definition: "One hand on the Word of God, the other on the student, bringing them together for life change."[5] This chapter gives an overall perspective on the life change expected in the lives of inmates and their families. Chapter 2 will focus on getting a hand on the Word — interpreting and applying the Scriptures with accuracy and diligence. Chapter 3 guides a greater understanding of the people being taught — hand on the student. Chapter 4 describes the power of the gospel in life change. Chapter 5 details how to faithfully fulfill our responsibilities to teach and care, providing the maximum opportunity for life change.

> One hand on the Word of God, the other on the student, bringing them together for life change.

Motivations for This Ministry

You and I Need Heart Change. A Malachi Dads prisoner/ministry leader at Angola shares this advice for potential small-group leaders, whether incarcerated or not: "The Lord has to change us first, then bring restoration to the next generation." So many times we hear stories of those working in prison ministries telling that *they* were the ones who had their own personal faith strengthened, their resolve to live for Christ heightened, or their love and leadership for their families magnified. Following a Returning Hearts weekend a guide said, "It was fantastic! I came home wanting to lead my family and live my life more fully." It should not be surprising how much the facilitator will grow as he or she serves in the Lifeline ministry.

Inmates Need Life Change. One of the most rewarding facets of prison ministry is seeing the transformation of a prisoner's life. Whether the facilitator has had the opportunity of leading the inmate to salvation in Christ or in a significant step of growth, it is quite motivating to be used of God in this way. Sadly, Christ-followers have not pursued this ministry. British prison ministry expert Gerard Crispin urges: "We should seek to pray for and reach with the gospel the worst of men and women, inside or outside prison. It is far better and God-honoring to throw away our prejudices, pray that prisoners will repent and be converted, and that — where possible (and sadly it is sometimes too late) — they approach victims humbly for their forgiveness and do what they can to express and evidence their sorrow over their sin. Pray that those who have offended our holy God and hurt others will yet live to be a blessing to others who otherwise might have been among their next victims."[6]

Society Needs Crime's Cycle Stopped. The admonition from the Scriptures shows how a changed life in Christ could also alter the community: *Let the thief no longer steal, but rather let him labor, doing honest work with his own hands, so that he may have something to share with anyone in need (Ephesians 4:28).*

The way a family, city, county, region, or nation is revived is by focusing on the spiritual needs. In describing victims of crime, Lampman and Shattuck said, "As much as our secular society and culture might suggest otherwise, we are, fundamentally, spiritual beings … When crime strikes, it causes a crisis and leaves a trail of wounded victims. These victims have needs — physical, financial, emotional, and spiritual."[7] Meeting spiritual needs will change a society's woes.

Within the first years of the Prison Fellowship® ministry, it had many critics. Charges of just another community program, Colson's attempt to restore his public image, "bored inmates taking advantage of hapless do-gooders … but after awhile they couldn't argue with the results."[8] Steve Humphreys, executive director of Focus Group Ministries, was motivated to launch a ministry to prisoners by visiting a relative: By his own description, Steve felt no compassion for prisoners. His attitude was that they had done the crime, so they should have to do the time. Convicted prisoners did not deserve his compassion. But when he visited his relative, what he saw changed his heart. He saw men with children on their laps, surrounded by family members, just ordinary men who happened to be dressed in stripped uniforms … he saw that prisoners are people who need and deserve God's grace as much as anyone.[9]

Believers Need to Obey the Lord. Jesus gave us this command: *So whatever you wish that others would do to you, do also to them, for this is the Law and the Prophets (Matthew 7:12).* A relative of an attendee in our Sunday morning adult Bible study group was tried and sentenced for a very serious crime. As the months and years passed, we prayed for his spiritual awakening, growth in Christ, protection, and possible parole and release. This is what we would want our church and fellowship group to do, to respond and support if one of our family members or friends were incarcerated. How thankful we were that a faithful witness in the prison in another state reached out to this lady's brother. Prison ministry is a command from Scripture (Hebrews 13:3).

Families Need Strength Building. While true of all families, the need for strengthening the home is never more acute than in an inmate's family. Factors of absence, separation, hurt, and pressures are weighty upon the functioning of a family (and often upon the inmate's mind). Prison ministry expert Henry G. Covert highlights just one of these factors: "Separation is most difficult when there are emergencies at home, including serious accidents, illnesses, or deaths. Some inmates experience multiple family deaths during their incarceration, and they must often grieve alone. Prisoners who are unable to attend funerals for financial, geographical, or security reasons experience feelings of intense guilt, isolation, and helplessness."[10]

The niche that the Lord has allowed for Lifeline to address these needs may seem indirect. However, families are beginning to be impacted via the prisoner's change of life and of heart.

Children Need Godly Parents. This is true whether the parent is present or absent (as in incarcerated) and being raised by a grandparent or another guardian. Those who have the most impact upon the child are those who live every day with them. The best way to fulfill the Great Commission, *make disciples of all nations (Matthew 28:19)*, may very well be to parent them in the home.[11] Parents are the most qualified to fulfill this task because of time, interest, investment, and connection. The evangelism and spiritual growth of children and youth is in the very DNA of the Awana Lifeline ministry.

Hindrances to This Ministry

Too Little Prayer — Too often we are prepared in every aspect but prayer. Our study, arrangements, planning, and fellowship are plentiful yet seemingly powerless. As we discussed principles for effective ministry at Angola, the inmates said, "Prayer makes the ministry!" Prayer changes our hearts. Prayer aligns us with the Holy Spirit. And of course prayer allows us to ask for the Lord's work in the lives of those we serve. "What the church needs today is not more machinery or better, not new organizations or more and novel methods, but men whom the Holy Ghost can use — men of prayer, men mighty in prayer."[12] Challenge Verse 1 (Acts 12:5) recounts how the church in Jerusalem prayed for the apostle Peter when he was incarcerated. They prayed that he would be released so that the gospel could be shared. We, as small-group leaders, should rally our churches to pray for the gospel to be shared so that prisoners would experience a spiritual releasing.

"Prayer makes the ministry!"

Need for Security — Prisons need to be secure places. Some outside volunteers may be tempted to forget this. Even now the memory of years ago being escorted into the Florida State Prison to conduct a Walk Thru the Bible™ live event brings a strong feeling of the double-security steel bars clanking shut! It was a reminder of the grace of God. I was at a high security prison all day — but there because a crowded chapel of inmates was gathered to learn about God and the Old Testament! What a mix of contrasts. In a place where some bad guys were being kept in prison, God had changed a host of men (and did so that day).

An outside volunteer needs to be aware of safekeeping measures. When items that are not allowed in the prison must be left outside the gate, it is for the good of all. When a wait to gain clearance to pass through security is enforced, it is for protection of people on the inside and out. The ignoring of security issues will result in a risk — either real or perceived — that cannot be tolerated. Respect for the safety of all should permeate the attitudes and actions of those involved in prison ministry.

Volunteers need to know what inmates know: Be vigilant and watchful. Some inmates will turn on you, manipulate you — they are skilled and good at this! Others are needy and can be very draining. You must be tough and tender. All inmate-students need protection from temptation to lie or deceive — just like you and me! Prison houses some individuals who are notorious and not safe.

Keep alert and aware of surroundings — even if they seem familiar. Prison officials seek to maintain authority for the safety of all.

Inmates need to be protected. When a volunteer asked a female inmate to write a note in her Hannah's Gift curriculum book, the prisoner wisely asked the warden for permission before she did so. Ministry is made possible when security is enforced at all times.

Guides (volunteers from outside or incarcerated) should be protected. Wearing clothing that is modest (and sometimes with specific regulations for attire) is important. Not bringing in materials or items that could be diverted to use as a weapon seems small, but is necessary. Being completely honest with prison officers helps maintain safety and proper order. Many factors can distract from a perfect setting for a Bible study or discussion. Seek to eliminate the distractions that you can, and live above the ones that can't be changed. Keep focused on the reasons you are there! Provide an opportunity for the growth of moms and dads in meeting Christ, growing in Him, and becoming life-giving parents.

Care to preserve confidentiality, proper respect for authority and procedures, and priority of the purposes of the ministry should be maintained at all times. *And whatever you do, in word or deed, do everything in the name of the Lord Jesus, giving thanks to God the Father through Him (Colossians 3:17)*, including the prison ministry.

Limited Time — The time orientation between those in prison and outsiders can become a hindrance. Usually inmates have time for thinking, reading, reflection, and study. "Prisons are all about time; and the Lord uses this sanctified hiatus to gather His tattered children to Himself and stiches their broken hearts with the golden threads of grace, love, and forgiveness."[13] But time for the guide may seem pushed and rushed. Seek to be as prepared as you can. Expect to be more flexible than you wish. Commit to be fulfilling the opportunity of the ministry that the Lord gives. *Look carefully then how you walk, not as unwise but as wise, making the best use of the time, because the days are evil (Ephesians 5:15-16)*.

Actions of This Ministry

Shepherding — It may sound funny to discuss this kind of leadership in the tough world of prison ministry. However, Peter's command to the elders is also a guideline for our ministry to inmates: *Shepherd the flock of God that is among you, exercising oversight, not under compulsion, but willingly, as God would have you; not for shameful gain, but eagerly; not domineering over those in your charge, but being examples to the flock (1 Peter 5:2-3).* What does shepherding look like? It is watching, providing the best environment for connection to Christ, the greatest possibilities for growth for which you can pray and plan. It is acting toward your small group as the Good Shepherd acts toward us (Psalm 23).

Friendship — The life-giving respect and mutuality of friendship may be difficult to express toward an inmate. The needs, the ever-present deceit and hardness, may be intimidating to the small group guide. However, it is essential that a tough bond of relationship be established. In the Old Testament, the encouragment of Jonathan and David toward each other is legendary (1 Samuel 18:1; 20:42). In the New Testament, when our Lord faced His sorrow before the cross, He called His three closest friends to watch with Him in prayer. We must work to establish this solid, guided type of relationship with the inmates we lead. The night before Chuck Colson went to prison he said, "To know love and friendship and to know in this cold and impersonal world there are people who care for each other as human beings, whether they're in the White House, a fellowship group, or a penitentiary, is a gift from God."[14]

METHOD: STORIES

The prophet Nathan had a difficult task! He had been sent by God to confront the king regarding his sins of adultery, deceit, abuse of power, and murder. Using a shepherd's tale, he incited the king to action and eventual repentance (2 Samuel 12:1-13). Stories are one of the primary means that Jesus used. The story has great power to move people toward obedience. Deuteronomy 6:20-21 even commands fathers to tell the story. "The Old Testament especially emphasizes storytelling as a method of communicating about God."[15] Storytelling can be life-changing. That's why we employ the story in facilitating prison ministry.

Overcoming the shortcomings of the schooling model, as Ivy Beckwith describes most of our educational ministry in her book *Formational Children's Ministry*, could benefit from the strength of the story. Crossing racial barriers also has a powerful base in telling the stories of successful leaders or living texts.[16] Timothy Paul Jones suggests living in God's story line as one of the most effective ways to disciple families.[17] Grant Horner, who teaches film as visual storytelling at The Master's College, contends, "Scripture does not call us to evacuate ourselves entirely from the pagan culture that surrounds us, but to use our wise and prudent interaction with that culture ..."[18]

Hearing Their Story

How does a facilitator put the story to good use with ministry to prisoners? Certain skills will be needed to employ stories in serving those in our prison ministry.

Listening — The ability to listen, to truly hear, is so important. Listening gives others permission to tell their story. Body posture, facial expression, and tone of voice all provide hints of the readiness to have others tell their story. When people feel that their personal stories have been heard, expectations for fellowship and growth are solidified. Discipleship mentors Jerry and Mary White share, "We often ask of our friends to tell us more of their stories, and it opens up hours of tears, laughter, and empathy as we develop our friendships. As we trade stories, we continue to learn about one another and gain new knowledge, appreciation, and understanding. We never fully escape our history."[19]

Drawing Out the Story — How can you get others to share their story? A dean from our school would often go around campus with this happy, yet inviting, question, "What's your story?" That is not a bad place to start! Simply asking others to tell us the events and meaning of their life experiences in a setting of care is strong ministry. Allow time to have each person in your group share their story. Invite others to enter into that understanding. Experienced leaders know that having others tell their story can be a powerful tool for evangelism and discipleship.

Christ's Life Shared — Growing up in a small church, we had regular occasions for publicly telling what Christ meant in our daily living during testimony time. When we share our story of life in Christ, others are encouraged! Our experiences form a common core of explanation for witness and mentoring. Lessons learned the hard way become the stepping stones for other members of our group.

Jesus told stories, usually in the form of parables. Stories taught new insights of wisdom, challenged unexamined areas of growth, corrected misdirected priorities, and prompted new steps of obedience. No wonder we often hear "the Bible is in fact a single Story that lays out a vision for the whole world."[20]

Learning to Tell Your Story

Sharing the gospel through storytelling is emphasized by Brian Godawa. He estimates that 30% of the Bible is propositional truth (rational, doctrinal presentation) and "70% is story and imagination (that is, narrative, metaphor, symbol, image, and poetry)."[21] Making an effort to develop the skills of storytelling may be a good use of time — and follows the biblical example.

What's your story?

STYLES OF STORIES

What story style should facilitators expect in their small groups? How does one craft and model sound storytelling techniques? Two experienced Christian educators discuss patterns for stories:

Usually a pattern is an archetype — a recurrent story pattern in literature. The most common archetypes are the quest, the journey, the death-rebirth motif, the initiation, tragedy (or the more specific pattern of the fall from innocence), the happy ending, crime and punishment, the temptation, and the rescue. The importance of identifying such patterns is that they allow us to see the story as a whole, not simply as a series of events that follow each other.[22]

Guided storytelling is used by experienced facilitators to enhance the life application in their small groups. Some leaders give up to 20 percent of their time to having guided storytelling. It's guided, because it is easy to allow the telling of life events to become disorganized, time-consuming, and ineffective. Here are several practical storying guidelines:

Chronology/Timeline — Perhaps the easiest way to articulate life events is to tell them in a sequence of happenings. If someone is 40 years old, you could prompt a sharing of one occasion from each of four decades of life.

Key Event — When Paul was sharing his defense, he recounted a specific time and place where he met Jesus personally (Acts 26:12-18). While this may be too threatening in the early stages of a group dynamic, it can be a deepening of understanding and care for the more experienced study.

Theme — Recounting a specific happening can focus rich story sharing. Usually the leader needs to first model the pattern and a key event from their own life. Care should be taken in the first person sharing as it can develop into a problem of too little time.

Combination — Using creativity in how you prompt inmates to tell their story becomes a matter of prayer and careful preparation. Building expectation in the group for the telling of life stories is important. Share with other group facilitators about their best practice. Read a broad perspective of materials, helping you to become a better storyteller and encourager of stories.

SOURCES OF STORIES

It would seem that with the love of people for storytelling — as evidenced in the interest of television, movies, and stage plays — we would not have difficulty in generating them. The following are a few reliable sources master group leaders have used.

Bible — The Scriptures recount the story of God intersecting with Israel and the Church throughout the Old Testament and the Gospels of the New Testament, making the Bible a strong source of stories for teaching.

Curriculum — The book for your small group may have excellent stories that illustrate, teach, warn, and motivate. Being wise in the use of these stories to promote conversation is an effective way to facilitate a small group.

History — Specific stories of life change in prison inmates abound, such as the one of Chuck Colson, founder of Prison Fellowship. Stories about chaplains Rick Sweeney, Morris Jackson, or Tom Beatty (all inmates at one time) and others are available. Our churches, the world, and any country or state will also give us historical events as rich accompaniments for teaching.

Personal Lives — The testimony — sharing what you have seen, heard, and experienced in Christ — may be one of the most door-opening stories you could tell. Who can argue with a well-crafted presentation of what you are an expert about — your own life! A caution is that we should be careful not to dominate every conversation with just our own personal experiences. Let others share their lives, their stories.

Imagination — The parables Jesus taught are a great example of imaginary stories. People's fascination with invented accounts can be attested to by the dollars and time spent in reading, viewing, or talking about fictional stories.

WHEN TO USE STORIES

Storytelling is not the only teaching method, but it is a good one. The story must fit the purpose of the teaching. Below are various ways to employ the story technique:

Group Building — Stories assist in getting acquainted, breaking the ice, and providing common ground for group dynamics.

Motivating — Sometimes hearing another person's inspirational account of living out their faith prompts us to develop endurance. *For whatever was written in former days was written for our instruction, that through endurance and through the encouragement of the Scriptures we might have hope (Romans 15:4).*

Challenging — When a direct answer might be too confrontational or harsh, a story can allow you to say the correction needed in a palatable way.

Instructing — Sometimes, especially for younger people, a story can teach more than a couple of pages of notes.

Goal Setting — When we hear the biographies of others who have attempted or believed great quests for God, we are given courage to set lofty goals ourselves.

Training — Learning to communicate with family members is a great use of storying. Just this skill alone might merit emphasis in the repertoire of teaching.

ORAL METHOD: STORYTELLING

Many people who are studying the Bible within our ministry do not have strong skills of reading. Is the use of storytelling a good way to serve them? Yes! "In fact, people were listening to the Bible being read aloud long before they had a private copy to read silently to themselves. In the ancient world people read aloud or listened as others read aloud. By some estimates, only about 15 percent of the general populace in the first century was literate."[23]

TEACHING POINTERS

Teach with variety. Every teaching principle does not need to have a story to illustrate it. As powerful as the story is, do not let it become mundane and mind-numbing. Storytelling is only one method. A variety of approaches will keep your learners engaged and alert. Speaking or singing in a monotone can become boring or even irritating. Don't let the teaching of God's Word become stale!

Teach with facilitation. Perhaps you have already noticed that we use the terms *guide* and *facilitator* when describing the small-group leaders for this ministry. Teaching with respect for the inmates' growth might necessitate that we limit our own conversation and storytelling. To be a successful teacher in prison ministry, seek to equip the moms or dads with the skills to lead their own families. Enable the discipleship that you are doing to be passed on to the next generation.

Teach by example. A professor from college days wanted us to set a passionate example for those we lead. Prison ministry is no exception to the power of a sound model. The love and service that Jesus demonstrated is also our call to a ministry of life change! *For I have given you an example, that you also should do just as I have done to you (John 13:15).*

Notes

[1] Lennie Spitale, *Prison Ministry: Understanding Prison Culture Inside and Out* (Nashville, TN: B & H Publishing Group, 2002), p. 190.

[2] Art Rorheim, *Fathers Again* (Streamwood, IL: Awana Clubs International, 2008), p. 10.

[3] Information is from the Awana Lifeline website at awanalifeline.org.

[4] Lawrence O. Richards, *Expository Dictionary of Bible Words* (Grand Rapids, MI: Zondervan, 1985), p. 443.

[5] Gregory C. Carlson, *Rock Solid Teacher: Discover the Joy of Teaching Like Jesus* (Ventura, CA: Gospel Light, 2006), pp. 8-9.

[6] Gerard Crispin, *Beyond Bars: Looking Inside the Inside Story* (Ryelands Road, Leominster, UK: Day One Publications, 2007), p. 20.

[7] Lisa Barnes Lampman and Michelle D. Shattuck, "Finding God in the Wake of Crime: Answers to Hard Questions," in *God and the Victim: Theological Reflections on Evil, Victimization, Justice, and Forgiveness*, (Grand Rapids, MI: William B. Eerdmans Publishing Co., 1999), pp. 2-3.

[8] John Perry, *God Behind Bars: The Amazing Story of Prison Fellowship* (Nashville, TN: W Publishing Group, 2006), p. 8.

[9] David W. Crocker, *The Samaritan Way: Lifestyle Compassion Ministry* (St. Louis: Chalice Press, 2008), p. 76.

[10] Henry G. Covert, *Ministry to the Incarcerated* (La Vergne, TN: Henry G. Covert, publisher, 2014), p. 28.

[11] See Rob Rienow, *Limited Church: Unlimited Kingdom; Uniting Church and Family in the Great Commission* (Nashville, TN: Randall House, 2013).

[12] E. M. Bounds, *The Complete Works of E. M. Bounds on Prayer* (Grand Rapids, MI: Baker Book House, 1990), p. 447.

[13] Spitale, *Prison Ministry: Understanding Prison Culture Inside and Out*, p. 260.

[14] As quoted by biographer Jonathan Aitken, *Charles W. Colson: A Life Redeemed* (Colorado Springs: Waterbrook Press, 2005), pp. 249-250.

[15] William R. Yount, *The Teaching Ministry of the Church*, 2nd ed. (Nashville, TN: B & H Publishing Group, 2008), p. 156.

[16] Jacqueline J. Lewis, *Power of Stories: A Guide for Leading Multi-Racial and Multi-Cultural Congregations* (Nashville, TN: Abingdon Press, 2008), p. 5.

[17] Timothy Paul Jones, *Family Ministry Field Guide: How Your Church Can Equip Parents to Make Disciples* (Indianapolis: Wesleyan Press, 2011), pp. 206-207.

[18] Grant Horner, *Meaning at the Movies: Becoming a Discerning Viewer* (Wheaton, IL: Crossway, 2010), p. 26.

[19] Jerry and Mary White, *To Be a Friend: Building Deep and Lasting Relationships* (Colorado Springs: NavPress, 2014), p. 62.

[20] J. Scott Duvall and J. Daniel Hays, *Living God's Word: Discovering Our Place in the Great Story of Scripture* (Grand Rapids, MI: Zondervan, 2012), p. 15.

[21] Brian Godawa, "Storytelling and Persuasion," in *Apologetics for a New Generation*, general editor Sean McDowell (Eugene, OR: Harvest House Publishers, 2009), p. 123.

[22] James C. Wilhoit and Leland Ryken, *Effective Bible Teaching,* 2nd edtion (Grand Rapids, MI: Baker Academic, 2012), p. 67.

[23] J. Scott Duvall and Hays, *Living God's Word: Discovering Our Place in the Great Story of Scripture*, p. 10.

KEY VERSES

Chapter 2

SCRIPTURE EQUIPS

*All Scripture is breathed out by God
and profitable for teaching,
for reproof, for correction,
and for training in righteousness,
that the man of God may be complete,
equipped for every good work.*

2 Timothy 3:16-17

Memory Verses

KEY VERSES

Scripture Equips

All Scripture is breathed out by God and profitable for teaching, for reproof, for correction, and for training in righteousness, that the man of God may be complete, equipped for every good work. (2 Timothy 3:16-17)

CHALLENGE VERSES 1

Jesus Fulfills Scripture

"The Spirit of the Lord is upon Me, because He has anointed Me to proclaim good news to the poor. He has sent Me to proclaim liberty to the captives and recovering of sight to the blind, to set at liberty those who are oppressed." And He began to say to them, "Today this scripture has been fulfilled in your hearing." (Luke 4:18, 21)

CHALLENGE VERSES 2

Interpreting Scripture

And behold, a lawyer stood up to put Him to the test, saying, "Teacher, what shall I do to inherit eternal life?" He said to him, "What is written in the Law? How do you read it?" (Luke 10:25-26)

Hand on the Word

BIG IDEA

The Word of God is the agent of change in people's lives. Consistent, meaningful study and obedience to the Scriptures is the basis of life change — faith in Christ and growth in Christ. **How do you read it?** is the essential question.

FOUNDATION

Ask yourself the question, Upon what do people depend to see their lives changed? Some would suggest good, solid repentance and change of thinking. Others would perhaps rely on a change of environment — a different setting for living. Good habits, intense effort and practice, friendships which hold them accountable, establishing goals, turning over a new leaf, a new program or lesson series, or any one of a number of other answers would surely have their place! However, if we are going to see real life change in people, we need

> We need to see the Spirit of God using the Word of God to do the work of God.

to see the Spirit of God using the Word of God to do the work of God. The Bible is the critical tool of the Holy Spirit in changing an inmate's life (or a leader's life).

How does life change happen? Through faith! Faith is the means that the Lord uses to make a person new in Christ. *So faith comes from hearing, and hearing through the word of Christ (Romans 10:17).* The word of truth is *the gospel of your salvation (Ephesians 1:13),* that is, it is the means that the Lord uses to bring a person to salvation (1 Peter 1:23).

And this faith through the Scriptures continues to demonstrate itself in the life of the believer. Our memory verses (2 Timothy 3:16-17) present several important understandings of the significance of Scripture:

Scripture is given by God. It is *breathed out by God.* As such, it is His breath, the very words He wanted us to have. It's not just a human book about God; but a divine book through human authorship that resulted in words on a page. The Scriptures were held, translated, and passed on to each generation so that the reader today has a reliable record of God's words. "God has given His people a sufficient revelation of Himself so that they are able to know, trust, and obey Him."[1]

Scripture is profitable for all. When you study the Bible, or help others do so, it can result in much benefit. The list of verses about the Scriptures at the end of this chapter may help you know just how valuable the Word is.

Scripture is active in the believer. The Bible says it is useful for *teaching* (knowing the truth for what life and faith should be), *reproof* (showing the error of behavior and moving a person toward the right path), *correction* (straightening wrong thinking, raising up the one who has fallen), and *training in righteousness* (guiding, disciplining and cultivating a godly lifestyle).

Scripture accomplishes a purpose in the believer. The Word in the Christ-follower prepares them to be complete in Christ and ready for good works (2 Timothy 3:17).

Because the Bible is such a special book, and given by God to us, we must be careful in how we learn from it, teach it, and plan to obey it. The ministry known as Awana[2] derived its name from this Bible verse: *Study to show thyself approved unto God, a workman that needeth not to be ashamed, rightly dividing the word of truth (2 Timothy 2:1, KJV).*

If we as teachers and facilitators are to handle the Scriptures rightly, we must first look at what the Bible is actually saying. And of course we want to obey and do what the Scriptures teach. But between these two steps of Bible study is that

> Awana –
> Approved workmen
> are not ashamed

of interpretation — understanding what the truth means. "Bible interpretation, then, as the second step in Bible study is absolutely essential. Interpretation is foundational to application. If we do not interpret properly, we may end up applying the Bible wrongly."[3] So how do we handle the Scriptures accurately and interpret correctly? What are the basic principles?

PRINCIPLES

If we are to get a good grasp on the Scriptures, a hand on the Word of God as we have been saying, we will have to interpret the Bible well. Some have given their entire lives to interpreting the Scriptures and admit they still don't have it all figured out. When guiding the study and application of the Bible, these seven principles form the basis of getting a firm grasp on the Word.

Normal — The Bible should be interpreted as any other book. Some people say *literal* instead of normal, but we know that God doesn't have feathers and a piece of fruit in His eye! When interpreting *Keep me as the apple of Your eye; hide me in the shadow of Your wings (Psalm 17:8)*, we know that the psalmist is using an illustration, an analogy. It's the normal understanding.

But too often we do something silly on the other side of the spectrum of handling the Scriptures. We assume that the clear, simple meaning cannot be the truth. For example, if you see/hear a report on the news of an accident between a dump truck and a car, you don't automatically change the truck into a bicycle! *Normally* we should take the meaning of the Bible in the same way. When speaking of this principle, a college professor was fond of saying, "If the first sense makes sense seek no other sense." If context, type of literature, logic, or the historical understanding suggests that the normal interpretation might not be the best, then consider a different meaning. But if the basic understanding is clear, don't seek to differ.

A student once asked during class, "Does this apply to miracles? Maybe the feeding of the 5,000 was really just an *example* of Jesus using the boy's lunch to teach gratefulness and sharing!" As a professor, I smiled. I told each one in the room to pull out their snack card and take a classmate to lunch. After that, I announced, "The professor did a miracle!" Ridiculous? Yes. Everyone knew that it was prompting sharing, not that I had ... *divided the two fish among them all (Mark 6:41).*

Author's Intention — A second principle focuses upon seeking to learn the author's (both divine and human) purpose in writing the words received. Sometimes, it is very clear to see what the author intends (John 20:30-31, 1 Timothy 3:14-15, 2 Peter 3:1). At other times, perhaps it is not so clear. Most commentaries and study Bibles include a purpose of the book section in their introduction. Why? To prepare the reader for a stronger grasp of the richness of what is being shared.

At times the writer of Scripture is *reporting* the events, principles, or reactions of people. But this does not mean he *approves* them! King David took the wife of Uriah as his own, and then covered it up, but reading the full context brings to light that this was a serious sin.

A young wife came to the church office to talk with me, her pastor. She had determined that she had married the *wrong* man (which being interpreted means she was thinking about another man as a better husband). In light of the verses that say a husband should love his wife and the wife should respect her husband, and the fact that neither of those were true in her marriage, well … our discussion went downhill from there, until we came back to what the apostle Paul might have really proposed (Ephesians 5:33). I am pleased to report that she has been happily married (after some repentance and restoration) to the *wrong* man for many years.

Scripture Interprets Scripture — The Bible will make its own message known. Too often when reading a verse that may not be clear, some of us immediately begin to determine the interpretation (often missing the true meaning). Keep reading! Many times the truth will be understood within the context. Or another passage will define and clarify the focus of your study. Biblical examples of this principle in action are when New Testament preachers apply Old Testament truth (John 10:34-38, Acts 2:16-21, Romans 1:17) and when the writers of the Chronicles describe the same events as those in 1 and 2 Samuel and 1 and 2 Kings.

The materials used in the Awana Lifeline ministry are intended to bring people into a clearer understanding of the Bible, not replace the Word. Often the answer to a question from an inmate can be answered with Scripture. This applies even if the question is about a verse of Scripture.

Grammatical — The *words* of Scripture and how they are used are very important in understanding the meaning of Scripture. If we believe that God has fully loaded the very words of the Bible with meaning, shall we not unload the interpretation for our growth? Looking at the definitions of the words (both in English and in the original languages — possible with software programs), the way that they are used and their flavorings will help the Bible study leader to know the meaning of Scripture in deep ways. Most words have a range of meaning which can be mined out by looking at synonyms (alternative words and expressions) and parsing (deconstructing the use and pattern of a word or phrase) action words, subjects, conjunctions, or prepositions. This sounds hard to do but it is worth the effort. Remember to put the meaning back together after you have torn a sentence or verse apart. Some group facilitators are great at presenting a buffet of meanings, but never really hand out any utensils. They talk on and on about the various understandings, but never summarize or bring specific steps of obedience to the surface.

It's true that grammar — the use of verbs, nouns, modifiers, phrases, and connectors — has fallen on tough times. Punctuation and the like do not seem as important in the days of text messaging and instant, abbreviated communication. However, Jesus seemed to think that the smallest alphabet letter of Scripture or tiniest indicator should not be neglected (Matthew 5:18).

A Bible student at the college where I taught didn't understand the meaning of 1 John. He then was encouraged to do a word study on several of the key terms. He reported such rich, deep learning that I was tempted to let him teach the class for an hour, sharing what an in-depth look at the words could do for the understanding of a chapter.

Contextual — We might understand this interpretation principle as very similar to the idea that Scripture interprets Scripture. Allow us to emphasize that the way to understand the message of the Bible is to interpret from the whole, that is, to place an individual principle under the observation of both the surrounding verses and the totality of the Bible. "The Scriptural context of every text is both immediate (the paragraph, chapter and book in which it is embedded) and distant (the total biblical revelation)."[4]

Historical — The setting in time is important if we are to comprehend the significance of a Bible verse, chapter, or book. You could ask the following question when seeking to determine the historical structure of a selection of Scripture: "What was the understanding in the lives of the human author and hearers?" You have to look at the cultural standards for morals, politics, family life, and other relationships. The society's perspective enables you to dig deeper into the meaning of a study. And don't just depend upon the author of your group curriculum. You may want to seek out a good study Bible, if possible. Also helpful are commentaries, Bible atlases, Bible dictionaries, or collections of historical explanations.

Care should be taken in interpretation to ensure that cultural and transcultural (relating across time and ages) understandings be clarified. There seems to be no such thing as noncultural principles. Even in the expression of meaning, we couch our words within our own societal language. John Stott calls this the original sense of Scripture and defines it in this way: "God chose to reveal Himself in precise historical contexts. Although His self-revelation is addressed to every person of every age and every country, each part of it was addressed in the first instance to a particular people of a particular age in a particular country. Therefore the permanent and universal message of Scripture can be understood only in the light of the circumstances in which it was originally given. It would obviously be very misleading to read back into Scripture the notions of a later age."[5]

A small-group Bible study was studying a popular Psalm sometimes called "The Shepherd Psalm." We determined that we would use the assistance of a scholar who had studied the life of shepherds during Biblical times.[6] The historical setting added much to the grasp of meaning.

Genre/Literature — The various kinds of writing (historical narrative, poetry, proverb, prophecy, epistle, etc.) assist the Bible student in knowing the meaning. Historical books are describing events and are different in approach than poetry books. The historical books of the Old Testament (Genesis through Esther) and the New Testament (the four Gospels and The Acts of the Apostles) generally recount facts about the people, places, and activities of characters in Bible times (although sometimes not in a chronological timeline). Poetry in the Old Testament is different from the poetry of today. "Hebrew poetry repeats and rearranges thoughts rather than sounds."[7] Proverbs are different than promises, prophecy from epistle (or letter). Knowing how the writing expresses thought is essential in knowing how to interpret that thought.

To handle the Scriptures in a sound way, the type of literature you are reading must be understood. For example, many people will take a proverb as a promise. A proverb is a wise saying "that is founded in the 'fear of the Lord', and that works out covenant life in the practical details of everyday situations and relationships."[8]

METHOD: QUESTIONS

The use of questions is one of the most effective and widespread teaching methods. The teachers in the Bible used questions, including our Lord Himself. The materials that you will be using for your facilitation of the group most likely will also employ questions. Let us ask several.

Q1: What is the best way to lead Lifeline small groups?

A: Small-group facilitators find that three different approaches have been effective:

The **question-by-question sequence** method follows the curriculum closely, using the questions in the book as the basis of the discussion. Leading in this way guarantees a full exposure to the materials, doesn't leave anything from the lesson out of the discussion and has the added benefit of allowing pretty tight accountability — it becomes obvious quite quickly if the inmate has not answered the questions in the book during their study. However, this tight sequencing, on occasion, does not allow for the flexing of available time, and priority issues are sometimes treated the same as simple knowledge questions.

Moving from unit to unit with a launching question, expanding question(s), and a summary question for each division of the lesson is the process used in the **section-summary** method. Launching questions initiate the discussion. Typically they are knowledge questions (see p. 39). Expanding questions seek to promote further participant interaction. These understanding questions (p. 40) bring the meaning of the study to the setting for all involved and prepare for application. Summary questions are almost always application-oriented in nature and are sometimes easy to neglect, yet so important for moving a student toward obedience. Application questions (described on p. 40) lead to specific plans and patterns of trust and obedience. The benefits include increased flexibility in timing and highlighting priorities, while still maintaining some strong connection to the lesson material.

The flow of **insight and application** questions is similar to the section-summary method, but involves the entire lesson. A launching question (carefully crafted) surveys the entire lesson, prioritizing the big idea and key issues. Insight (understanding) questions assist in interpreting specific steps of growth. Application questions set the faith steps that the student would want to take. Each one establishes a specific action plan for following the Lord. This method allows for maximum flexibility in timing and priority issues and is more focused in moving toward mutual sharing of goals and control between inmates and leaders. It draws out a richer fellowship among participants and requires a prepared, somewhat skilled, and confident leader to be successful.

Q2: What are some of the biggest hindrances to good group dynamics?

A: Some major hindrances are a leader who controls too much of the discussion, lacking creative inviting questions, boredom, and not knowing how to follow a facilitator's process of guiding. Effective leaders share control with their group. They are confident and ready for the Holy Spirit to use them to prompt the inmate toward faith and specific steps of submission to Christ. Creative questions are discussed on the next page. Boredom may be hard to overcome. External circumstances that hinder interaction sometimes

cannot be avoided. However, the leader's internal attitude of passion for the Lord prompts enthusiasm in the group; it's contagious. Also, removing any barriers (that you can) to good learning will assist
in combatting boredom. Thinking about more than just the subject, developing wise compassion for each student and above all, thinking and planning for the style or delivery of the lesson are boredom busters.

Q3: What is meant by facilitator's process of guiding?

A: Some goals include:

- A leader who knows how to use knowledge, understanding, and application questions

- A leader who avoids asking too many questions, therefore allowing for the inmates' maximum progress towards responsive obedience

- A leader who overcomes his or her own nervousness to serve the inmates

More specific how-tos are presented in Chapter 5. Another key action of the guiding process is using connector comments.

Connector comments

When you ask a solid question (one that has more than one answer, makes people think, guides toward mutual discussion, etc.) but then pile on another question before people have had a chance to think, that is bypassing a sound process. Connector comments are either short questions or affirmations or even gestures which prompt continued discussion. These comments can apply to all the approaches as listed above in Question 1. A few examples are:

- "OK, good answer. What else?"

- Repeat the main question again for additional answers.

- "Anyone else?"

- "Yes."
- "Good point."
- "Tell us more!"
- Build on another participant's answer by asking others to comment.

Q4: What should be accomplished in using questions?

A: Some goals include:

- Not just covering the material, but deep knowledge

  Gain a thorough grasp of what the author of the lesson book and the Lord of the Scriptures would have each one know.

- Not just knowing the information, but broad understanding

  There needs to be a significant spiritual difference between your study and the book club. We are guiding people toward a response to relationship with Christ.

- Not just explaining the lesson, but personal application

  Eventually a group member must move from understanding what the lesson means to a process of using the information for their own life (and the lives of their family).

Q5: What types of questions should I be asking?

A: The Evangelical Training Association's book *Understanding Teaching* includes this full description of the types of questions that should be used in guiding a small-group Bible study.

Knowledge Question(s) — These launching questions take students back to the text to discover what the Bible says. Guidelines:

- The knowledge question should have several correct answers.
- You should be able to connect a verse reference to support the answer.

- Be careful not to be too specific or narrow in your knowledge questions.

- There may be more than one right answer.

- One of the obvious answers should lead to an area of understanding.

- Avoid asking too many knowledge questions.

Understanding Question(s) — These questions should guide a student to interpret what a Bible passage means. Guidelines:

- Understanding questions should flow from the knowledge section.

- Understanding questions should promote discussion.

- Avoid short, obvious questions or yes or no questions.

- Try to put the meaning in everyday, practical terms.

Application Question(s) — These questions should lead a student in applying the meaning of a Bible passage. Students should be able to answer, "What does this mean to me/us?" Guidelines:

- Application questions are based upon a relational setting with the group.

- Applications should be based upon the study that preceded it.

- Don't try to apply too many things.

- Identify with a specific time frame — such as today, this week, or by next Thursday.[9]

ORAL METHOD: ASKING QUESTIONS

How can questions assist in the teaching of those with limited reading skills? In the church, questions have been used by biblical teachers and Christian educators for centuries. Following are some examples:

Supports the learning process — Jesus demonstrated the use of questions in His teaching. When training the disciples, He used rhetorical questions (Luke 9:25). When seeking to surface the attitudes of the learner's heart, He used questions (Luke 11:40). As a follow-up to other methods, such as storytelling, Jesus would often use questions (Luke 7:42-47). We, as small-group leaders, may find that those who struggle with reading or learning will profit from questions which build understanding, clarify responses, lead to deeper reflection, and prompt faith-oriented action plans.

Catechism — Some Christian teachers have used this structured form of questions in their teaching. A specified set of questions is prepared, and the learners recite and repeat till the answers are memorized. Although some would say this method is an invitation to boredom, others vigorously support this effective way of learning.

Preschooler learning — If you have ever spent time working with a very young child, you know the power (and sometimes frustration) of questions. A teacher-in-training observed a 4- year-old and his parent. The young one asked over one hundred questions in five minutes. It seems to be the primary way to learn for this age group.

Socratic method — Leading a student to conclusions by asking questions is another very effective method. It can be manipulative, but sometimes it proves to be a very quick and pointed way to grasp understanding and insight.

Guiding with questions — The conversations that we often have with students before and after class sessions are sometimes more remembered than our lessons! Knowing how to ask questions that lead to mutual sharing is a skill of the master teacher. Guided conversation can profit both student and teacher.

VERSES ABOUT THE SCRIPTURES
Following are verses that highlight the power and impact of the Scriptures. The order of the references is according to their sequence in the Bible. The Word:

- Is the basis for ministry to the next generations when in the heart (Deuteronomy 6:4-9).

- Guides toward good and profitable journeying in God (Joshua 1:8).

- When meditated upon, produces a person in direct contrast to the wicked (Psalm 1).

- Changes the life of the follower of God in so many ways (Psalm 19:6-11).

- Is applauded in almost every one of the 176 verses. Several favorites are verses 9 and 11, describing the power of the Scriptures to keep a young person from sin, verse 105, telling us that the Bible is a light for our way, and verse 165, informing us of the peace that comes to the believer in loving the Word (Psalm 119).

- Accomplishes the Lord's will in the proper season (Isaiah 55:10-11).

- Is the joy in the life of the believer (Jeremiah 15:16).

- Is what Jesus used to overcome Satan's temptations (Matthew 4:4, 7, 10).

- Will be fulfilled in every aspect (Matthew 5:18).

- Shows a person Christ (even the Old Testament!) (Luke 24:27, 45).

- Bears witness that Jesus is the Savior (John 5:39).

- Makes a person free! (John 8:31-32).

- Is the way to love, know, and grow in Christ (John 14:21).

- Is the path of fruitfulness and power in prayer (John 15:7-8).

- Sanctifies (makes a person holy) in the truth (John 17:17).

- Builds up in faith (Acts 20:32).

- Instructs toward endurance and hope (Romans 15:4).

- Is the power of God (1 Corinthians 1:18).

- Cleanses from sin (Ephesians 5:26).

- Protects and gives strength to fight spiritual battles (Ephesians 6:17).

- Gives ability to endure and hold on to hope (Philippians 2:16).
- Is the basis of teaching and admonishing (Colossians 3:16).
- Prompts believers to live lives worthy of God (1 Thessalonians 2:12-13).
- Reproves (turns toward the right path), rebukes (shows the error of a person's way), and encourages (2 Timothy 4:2).
- Becomes the standard of conduct (Titus 2:5).
- Judges (or discerns) thoughts and intents of the heart (Hebrews 4:12).
- Causes spiritual growth (1 Peter 2:2).

TEACHING POINTERS

Teach for connection. Of course we hope that support and fellowship with others in the group occurs; but here we are really talking about a relationship with God. We'll say more about this in Chapter 4 (Gospel of Grace), but how tragic that an inmate would know so much about the Lord but never know Him.

Teach for meaning. Too many times Bible study can become just a discussion of ideas without anyone responding to the Lord. "Your quest is for meaning. Unfortunately, too much Bible study begins with interpretation, and furthermore, it usually ends there."[10] Become passionate about moving your students toward obedience. Don't allow your people to miss seeing in the Word the truth that God has given. Don't allow your group to fall short of application.

Teach expecting the Holy Spirit to make the Word clear and effective. He is the Teacher, we are His assistants. Evangelist Bill Fay counsels, "There will be no argument or negative exchange. Why? Because you aren't pressing your interpretation. The Holy Spirit does all of the convicting. You are in the page turning business at this point. Your one goal is to stay out of God's way."[11]

Notes

1 Lane T. Dennis, Executive Ed., "The Bible and Revelation," *ESV Study Bible, English Standard Version* (Wheaton, IL: Crossway, 2008), p. 2508.

2 More information about Awana is available at <u>awana.org</u>.

3 Roy B. Zuck, *Basic Bible Interpretation* (Colorado Springs: Cook Communications Ministries, 1991), p. 14.

4 John Stott, *Understanding the Bible* (Grand Rapids, MI: Baker Books, 1984, 2001), p. 152.

5 Ibid, p. 147

6 W. Phillip Keller, *A Shepherd Looks at Psalm 23* (Grand Rapids, MI: Zondervan, 1997).

7 Lawrence O. Richards, *The Teacher's Commentary* (Wheaton, IL: Victor Books, 1987), pp. 325-326.

8 Lane T. Dennis, Executive Ed., "Introduction to Proverbs," *ESV Study Bible, English Standard Version* (Wheaton, IL: Crossway, 2008), p. 1130.

9 Gregory C. Carlson, "Preparing Yourself in the Word," *Understanding Teaching* (Wheaton, IL: Evangelical Training Association, 1998), Instructional Resource Guide, Worksheets 9 & 10.

10 Howard Hendricks, *Living By the Book* (Chicago: Moody Press, 1991), p. 35.

11 William Fay and Ralph Hodge, *Share Jesus Without Fear* (Nashville, TN: LifeWay Press, 1997), p. 35.

Chapter 3

MINISTER TO THE LEAST OF THESE

*And when did we see You sick
or in prison and visit You?
And the King will answer them,
"Truly, I say to you, as you did it
to one of the least of these
My brothers, you did it to Me."*

Matthew 25:39-40

Memory Verses

KEY VERSES

Minister to the Least of These

And when did we see You sick or in prison and visit You? And the King will answer them, "Truly, I say to you, as you did it to one of the least of these My brothers, you did it to Me." (Matthew 25:39-40)

CHALLENGE VERSE 1

Heart in View

For the LORD sees not as man sees: man looks on the outward appearance, but the LORD looks on the heart. (1 Samuel 16:7b)

CHALLENGE VERSES 2

Encouragement in Christ

So if there is any encouragement in Christ, any comfort from love, any participation in the Spirit, any affection and sympathy, complete my joy by being of the same mind, having the same love, being in full accord and of one mind. Do nothing from selfish ambition or conceit, but in humility count others more significant than yourselves. Let each of you look not only to his own interests, but also to the interests of others. (Philippians 2:1-4)

Hand on the Student

BIG IDEA

Building a relationship with the people in your sphere of influence (small group) to guide and facilitate faith and spiritual growth is the environment for life change, both in the inmates' lives and in those of their families. **What does this person need?** is the relational question.

FOUNDATION

Serving the Least of These — The biblical foundation for ministry to the prisoner cannot be neglected. Our memory verses for this chapter have a focus on the ministry to inmates. Jesus' words ***as you did it to one of the least of these*** *(Matthew 25:40*, emphasis added) shows that God indeed has a heart for the incarcerated person. Who are those in prison and how should we visit them?

The prison population in the United States at the end of 2012 was reported at 2,228,400 persons (one of every 108 residents) with nearly seven million adults supervised by the correctional systems (about one of every 35 residents).[1] The National Prisoner Statistics Program collects data by government mandate regarding those prisoners incarcerated, including information regarding sex, race, non-U.S. citizenship, etc., individuals on probation or parole, and reports via various instruments. One such report is from the U.S. Department of Justice Bureau of Justice Statistics. These numbers may present pressing needs in the inmate population, but another hidden population is also impacted: the families of the incarcerated person. "It is difficult for inmates to believe that supportive friends and relatives can become distant, independent, or even hostile … they fail to understand how their incarceration affects others."[2]

Pursuing Goals With Hope for the Heart — Complicated issues of prisoner rehabilitation, prison reform, and society transformation are worthy objectives. However, with these complex issues, we must keep a priority focus. The final outcome of any ministry, perhaps especially prison ministry is *Christ in you, the hope of glory. Him we proclaim, warning everyone and teaching everyone with all wisdom, that we may present everyone mature in Christ (Colossians 1:27b-28).* Hope is a powerful goal to pursue in the ministry of those incarcerated. "In God's revelation of Himself to sinful men and women, He always gives hope! Can Christians, then, remain idle while those with whom we share the same sinful nature are stripped of hope?"[3]

A change of heart is what is needed! The prophet tells us: *The heart is deceitful above all things, and desperately sick; who can understand it? (Jeremiah 17:9).* We see evidence of this not only in the prison system, but in society and in our own lives. The heart is "the center of life, thought, feeling, and even spiritual response … the center of one's spiritual perception and purpose … the central point of people, that point where the emotions,

Heart change

reasoning, spiritual instincts, and God-consciousness is."[4] As the small-group facilitator seeks to pray and prepare so that the visit they have includes a heart change, it is entirely appropriate to pray for these deeper level aims. We, as humans, may look at the outside of the prisoner but God looks at the heart (1 Samuel 16:7b). Christian educator Gary Newton shares that heart-deep learning goals keep both teacher and student reflecting and applying the Scriptures to life.[5]

Viewing Relationships as God Does — Relationships are impacted! Family members, friends and even the inmates' own perspectives can become distant and dark. An emphasis on the Scriptural command to *count others more significant than yourselves (Philippians 2:3* from the Challenge Verses) is only a reflection of God's love for us. That is the basis of being able to love a prisoner. We must consider that the inmate is a person who is loved by God. *And you, who once were alienated and hostile in mind, doing evil deeds, He has now reconciled in His body of flesh by His death, in order to present you holy and blameless and above reproach before Him (Colossians 1:21-22).* Changing our mindset to view the prisoner as God does may take some adjustment. Angela Yuan is the mother of Christopher Yuan, a current Moody Bible Institute instructor and former inmate. She describes her observation of watching incarcerated men meet with their loved ones during visitation and reflects on some of her own attitudes. "In the past, I had thought that prison inmates were the worst people imaginable: murderers, rapists, thieves, gangsters … monsters. But now, as we stood watching families reunited, I realized that these men were not monsters. Standing before me were fathers, brothers, husbands, and sons."[6]

Developing Perspectives of Ministry — What might be some key activities or attitudes that a group facilitator would aspire towards to prompt and motivate? As servants of Christ, we want to establish an environment for spiritual growth beyond just the meeting in the group. A couple of these activities/attitudes are:

• Bible Reading

  If the inmate is going to grow in Christ, there must be an intentional, consistent exposure to and application of the Word of God. Describing the life change that happened in Charles Colson, Watergate figure, prisoner, and founder of Prison Fellowship Ministries, the biographer highlights his devotional life. Responding to Colson's question about ministerial burnout among those who serve the gospel, the Reverend Neal Jones, friend and mentor responded: "Build yourself a strong devotional discipline with Bible reading at the heart of it."[7] A worthy goal of a small-group facilitator is to prompt a consistent devotional time, especially emphasizing the reading of the Scriptures. Often this spiritual discipline is called a quiet time, but let us label it an appointment with God — a time that one might look forward to, just as with any set-aside time with a friend.

- Prayer

  The spiritual discipline of prayer is both a practice and an action for the inmate (and for those who guide them!). Prayer connects the incarcerated person with their Lord and gives an outlet for deep connection with Christ. The Holy Spirit is able to prompt prayer in the most desperate of persons (Romans 8:26). Prayer is like breath to the Christian walk. It is more than asking, but certainly includes this in the relationship we have with the Father. Jesus encouraged us to pray. *Until now you have asked nothing in My name. Ask, and you will receive, that your joy may be full (John 16:24). You do not have, because you do not ask (James 4:2).* Prayer is a personal and group discipline that moves us toward a stronger relationship with the Lord.

Other spiritual disciplines can certainly be applied to the growth of a believer in Christ. But staying with the basics of Bible study/ meditation and prayer are normal and practical to model and train.

PRINCIPLES

Salvation Needed — Perhaps this need not be emphasized in prison ministry, but it is too easy to be caught up in meeting needs, arranging for security, planning a lesson, and being prepared that we miss the foundation and force for life change — the gospel! The apostle Paul said it is *... the power of God for salvation to everyone who believes ... (Romans 1:16).* The gospel is so essential in prison ministry that an entire chapter of this book is devoted to the topic (see Chapter 4).

The gospel is the message of salvation by grace through faith (Ephesians 2:8-9). Our ministry should keep primary the sharing of the gospel. It is grace in action. When the gospel is believed, that person becomes a new creation (2 Corinthians 5:17). This is life change that is not temporary and insecure but eternal.

Issues Inmates Face — To begin to describe the needs of inmates is a formidable task. Numerous issues could be addressed as a guide thinks of the inmates in the small group. Experts who have been involved in prison ministry for years have ably addressed the adjustments and stresses prisoners face. However, a few crucial issues may be mentioned here to highlight the culture that exists for the inmate.

• Loneliness seems so strong; it certainly results from the sepa-ration that is experienced. Being in a new and strange place where your schedule and activities are not under your control is scary enough. But then to have your familiar support system gone (or at the minimum distant) leaves the inmate with intense feelings of missing family and friends. Perhaps this is a great op-portunity for ministry, where an entrance for relationship leading to the gospel can happen. A next-door neighbor who was in-carcerated during the years our sons were in elementary school was surprised when we attempted to go through the process of being on his list of approved visitors. It was not that the list was too full, but he was amazed we wanted to be on it!

• Accountability would seem built-in to prison life. Paying the debt to society surely includes being held accountable for crimes committed. However, each individual needs personal account-ability to God and to self (and often others) if they are going to grow in Christ. Realizing the impact of sin upon our world is one thing, but understanding one's own personal responsibility is another. Experienced prison ministry director Lennie Spit-ale recounts how a female inmate was sobbing, not able to be comforted by the other inmates. She kept saying "I didn't know it was wrong! I didn't know it was wrong!" Later it was discovered she was referring to her involvement in prostitution. Spitale summarizes, "She knew that it was a criminal act as far as the state was concerned, but she had never thought about it as being a sin against a personal God."[8] David, when confronted with his adultery and murder, repents by saying he has sinned against God (Psalm 51:4). To be a Christ-follower in growing well or long, one must submit to friend and/or authority. Accountability is God's instrument of shaping in sanctification, making us aware of our need for Christ and encouraging us to respond to Him.

- Forgiveness is precious. In Christ, we have been strengthened so that we can endure, qualified so that we can share in the inheritance, delivered from the domain of darkness so that we can live in the kingdom of the Son, and redeemed (bought with a price) so that we can have forgiveness of sins (Colossians 1:11-14). How does forgiveness become evident? As a person believes, forgiveness from God begins to be real from the moment the Father transacts it. The blood of Christ provides this standing (1 Peter 1:18-21). Forgiveness from others is also valuable and at times the greatest indication of Christ's work in the life of a believer. While attending a Christian college in Omaha, the buildings and grounds director made a huge impact on the community. He and his wife weekly visited the man in jail who had murdered one of their two young sons and maimed the other. The purpose was to extend forgiveness. Unbelievable! The Lord used that forgiveness to lead many to Himself.

But perhaps one of the more difficult undertakings is to forgive oneself! How often have you heard the phrase, "I just can't forgive myself!?" The current director of chaplains for Good News Jail and Prison Ministry was a student at the college where I was a professor. In meeting with him in conversation, it became clear that as Rick experienced the love and forgiveness Christ had extended (he was a former inmate), he could forgive himself and then go about sharing the gospel with others. It was life changing! We can forgive ourselves not because we deserve it or have earned it, but because of the work of Christ.

Family Connection/Restoration — The pressing need for inmates, especially those who are parents, is for a connection and restoration with their families. The "Malachi Dads Pledge" and "Hannah's Gift Pledge"[9] highlight this important aspect of an inmate's life. The situation at home is often on the hearts and minds of an inmate. The fact is that family life has to continue on the outside. The inmate's family now has the disruption of the incarceration. That family is adjusting and experiencing stresses and needs just as strong as the inmate. Knowledge of the pain caused by the incarceration is often a crushing blow. That is why the ministry you are doing is doubly crucial! Not only are you ministering to the inmate, but also to his or her family.

The needs of these families might be quite obvious. Absence of a father or mother, perhaps having different living circumstances, and already existing strains are intensified. Finances are even more limited, discipline for children more challenging. Deeper and more subtle influences arise: "Family members describe incarcerations as pitting material interests against the social norms of kinship, a conflict that contributes to a host of behaviors within families that are at once rational, socially destructive, and painful. They describe how incarceration encourages infidelity, distrust, abuse, and neglect.[10] Prison inmates and their families value the ties that are associated with kinship. However, these values are difficult to live out. The incarcerated person's family has many similarities to families in urban, economically depressed areas. "Extensive research indicates that men, women, and children in poor neighborhoods value family no less than do other Americans but face considerably greater obstacles in maintaining familial integrity."[11] How can we assist the inmate in building or restoring family relationships?

One of the first adjustments which needs to be made is to clarify and establish the new role of the parent (or spouse, child, sibling, etc.). Identifying who they are in relationship to the family may be hard work for the inmate. Perhaps decisions, actions, or even abuse have marred the interaction with the outside family members. And the fact of incarceration has compounded the resentment and hurt. To meet these challenges, the inmate must have a relationship with Christ and become a new person. Both *Malachi Dads: The Heart of a Father* and *Hannah's Gift: The Heart of a Mother* emphasize the life change that faith in Christ creates *before* trying to be a better parent. We can tell inmates: "If you are changed in your life with Christ, then your family will eventually see that change!"

The incarcerated person will then have to learn how to "parent from a distance." This is hard work! It will take time, energy, patience, and faith in the Lord. One father participating in the Malachi Dads program at Louisiana State Penitentiary (also known as Angola) waited for years until his son was ready to attend a

Returning Hearts event. When he did, it was great. But as we spoke together years later, he was still praying for a second opportunity of personal interaction with his son. Effort and creativity will need to match this investment of time. As a volunteer going into the prison, you will find from other peers and the inmates themselves the best practices and sustaining attitudes which extend the hope of connection in Christ's name to the inmate's family. Perhaps the biblical admonition applies especially to a dad or a mom who is seeking to parent: *And let us not grow weary of doing good, for in due season we will reap, if we do not give up (Galatians 6:9).*

Parent from a distance

Hannah, in the Old Testament, is the example whom Dr. Kristi Miller used as the basis for her book for prison moms. She cautioned, "Parenting is different for the incarcerated mom! Tell the moms: 'Your role is still God-given!'"[12] She shared several other differences that the female prison mom faces:

1. When a mom is imprisoned, someone else has to step in. This is often different than for dads. With a mom leaving, a relative, friend, or a child protection home is called upon to care for the child(ren). This may come with bitterness from the caregiver, which in turn will influence the child.

2. A mother is drowning in her own guilt (and sometimes anger). The maternal instincts can crush a prison mom with remorse. Frustration about the lack of ability to address the situation can result. That is why an incarcerated mother must have a growing relationship with the Lord and prayer support from her group. This is not an easy hurdle to overcome.

3. For some reason, children seem quicker to forgive and admit or allow mistakes in the relationships with their dad. This resentment between a mom and her child(ren) must be faced, forgiveness sought, and relationships established. God is able to make grace abound.

Moms and dads everywhere know the challenges of normal parenting. The foundation for any success lies in the commitment of the parent to Christ, allowing grace, love, hope, and faith to flow through them. The first parenting step is to begin (and mend) sound communication. When communication is established and growing, understanding will result. When understanding (the ability to see what the other person sees and feel what the other person feels) is occurring, then acceptance (allowing God to change the person's attitude) and trust (the safety to add personal effort to the relationship) will build and create a situation where close family fellowship grows.

The inmate who wants to become the godly parent faces barriers in establishing a relationship with his or her family. External forces such as distance, safety for the child, arrangements for time and opportunity, along with communication frustrations, can seem overwhelming. Caregivers, who often are sacrificing greatly because of the incarceration of the mom, are reluctant to facilitate a renewed relationship with the child. Perhaps because of the damage caused by the incarcerated parent or fear in various forms, the effort to overcome these external factors isn't enough. A Returning Hearts[13] coordinator shared about her sorrow in seeing numerous Malachi Dads participants whose children did not come to the celebration. It broke her heart to know that these dads were ready for a visit, but the bus didn't come to pick up the kids in the city or that the promised ride for the kids forgot!

Sometimes the parent doesn't see their child because the kids are still working through the internal barriers. Past hurts, mistrust from broken promises, deception of the past, and fear in its various forms all contribute to hindering family faith relationships. The remedy is to become a godly person, by the power of the Holy Spirit, receiving the grace of God and extending that grace to others.

What does an inmate need? Some of the most crucial issues that face an incarcerated parent are humility, genuine life-changing faith, anger management, understanding drug and alcohol influence, conflict resolution, stress, being a distant parent, components of relationships that are sound, pornography and masturbation, the importance of chastity, how to be a parent, discipline in the home, and resources for surviving on the outside of prison.[14] An important principle to remember: The life transformation we pray and work for is not from a social agenda, but a soul-changed faith in Christ. The power for a life transformed is in the sanctifying work of the Holy Spirit. *And such were some of you. But you were washed, you were sanctified, you were justified in the name of the Lord Jesus Christ and by the Spirit of our God (1 Corinthians 6:11).*

> Life transformation ... is not from a social adenda, but a soul-changed faith in Christ.

METHOD: CONVERSATION

One powerful avenue that builds understanding of inmates and their families is conversation. It is "an exchange of information, ideas, and opinions and requires two-way communication consisting of listening and oral expression."[15] Conversation — the dialogue between individuals and groups — is a method and skill set which fosters an environment for life change.

Dialogue — To effectively have a conversation, it should be guided, i.e., "informal but planned dialogue."[16] Listening should be practiced and patience in it pursued. Learning to be brief yet clear will also help conversation. How should we be involved in conversation?

- Heart check — talk to your own soul. The psalmist does this (Psalm 42:5)! It is entirely appropriate to have a talk with yourself, open to the Lord about the issues that you face. Some might call this audio thinking as it allows for your thoughts and emotions to focus. This contemplation will strengthen you in Christ and your commitment to the ministry with inmates.

- Prayer — converse with the Lord. Prayer cannot be emphasized too much. A conversation with the Lord — Brother Lawrence calls this " the practicing of the presence of God" — is combined with specific, intentional prayer practices. Prayer should be a common conversational practice of teacher and student.

- Respect — listen to authorities. Administrators, guards, and chaplains have valuable insights into how to effectively carry out the ministry to inmates. Each authority may have differing perspectives, but a wise facilitator gathers understanding and proper procedures from listening to and talking with those in authority.

- Facilitation — interact with inmates/students. Talking with the inmates in the group would seem like it would not have to be emphasized. Yet too many times a guide will have a one-way conversation — which is really not a conversation at all. The minutes before, after, and during group time are valuable for setting an environment of care and shepherding. The experienced group leader takes advantage of these windows of insight. "Planning in opportunities for talking about meanings and experiencing of truth, voicing fears, and sharing questions with one another prepares the ground for new formation to occur."[17]

Listening — Perhaps the more difficult side of a conversation is listening! Trying to co-lead a Bible study once with the other leader and three others of the eight-person group continually talking caused for a running dialogue with no-one listening! The groups that are the most effective will have leaders who know how to practice listening and how to guide listening for everyone involved.

- Learn to Listen — When I have pause to review my listening skills, I try to note how much of the conversation is focused on my words. If I am dominating the dialogue, then I intentionally seek to give others the opportunity to share. I do this by waiting before I ask too many questions, allowing silence as individuals think through their responses. I also prompt those members who perhaps have been overshadowed in the conversation.

- Ask Good Questions — The skill of asking great questions (highlighted in Chapter 2) makes conversation happen. Planning and practicing the art of asking sound questions are strong aspects of readiness to listen.

- Observe — Professor and small-group expert Bill Donahue shares how guides need to listen to the nonverbal messages like "facial expressions, tone of voice, and body movements and posture."[18] Becoming an observant facilitator will make you a great leader.

ORAL METHOD: CONVERSING

You don't need to be able to read to have great conversations! The deep interaction of a personal dialogue has far-reaching impact. The teachings of Christ, while written down for us in the Scriptures, were often in response to interchange with an individual. Examples include relationships with His family (Matthew 12:46-50), a pointed discussion with religious leaders about taxes — doesn't that sound contemporary? — (Mark 12:13-17), and with a scholarly seeker (Mark 12:28-34).

Conversing is a strong avenue to share spiritual development in our ministries. Timothy Keller describes conversation and its effect in his church. "Gospel renewal in the church spreads through renewed individuals talking informally to others. It is in personal conversations that the gospel can be applied most specifically and pointedly."[19] Conversation can have the same impact in our prison ministry.

TEACHING POINTERS

Teach with reserve. Coming from a farm background during my growing up years, the following principle when feeding cattle (and probably it applies to leading group studies) is understood: "Don't dump the whole haystack!" Even Jesus, the Master Teacher, told His disciples: *I still have many things to say to you, but you cannot bear them now (John 16:12).*

Teach with mutuality. Mutuality is the ability to share control and guide a study without dominating or hindering participation. What we want to achieve in our small groups is a "student-centered, teacher-guided"[20] style.

Teach with confidence. What if you don't feel adequate to lead the study? You are in good company! Neither did Paul (2 Corinthians 3:5-6). That is why we move on in faith, knowing that the Lord Jesus has qualified us for the life (1 John 2:28-29) and ministry (2 Corinthians 3:4-6) we have. "God has revealed a sufficient knowledge of His love and grace for believers to have both faith and hope in Him, and be assured that if Christians study the Bible, not with prejudice and criticism, but with faith in and love for its Author, they will understand its message."[21]

Notes

1. Lauren E. Glaze and Erinn J. Herberman, "Correctional Populations in the United States, 2012," *Bureau of Justice Statistics Bulletin* (U.S. Department of Justice, Office of Justice Programs, December 2013, www.ojp.usdoj.gov), pp. 2-3.

2. Henry G. Covert, *Ministry to the Incarcerated* (Chicago: Loyola Press, 1995), p. 21.

3. Paul D. Schoonmaker, *The Prison Connection* (Valley Forge, PA: Judson Press, 1978), p. 81.

4. Wayne A. Detzler, *New Testament Words in Today's Language* (Wheaton, IL: Victor Books, 1986), pp. 206-207.

5. Gary Newton, *Heart-Deep Teaching: Engaging Students for Transformed Lives* (Nashville, TN: B & H Publishing Group, 2012), p. 99.

6. Angela and Christopher Yuan, *Out of a Far Country* (Colorado Springs: WaterBrook Press, 2011), p. 156.

7. Jonathan Aitken, *Charles W. Colson: A Life Redeemed* (Colorado Springs: Waterbrook Press, 2005), pp. 340-341.

8. Lennie Spitale, *Prison Ministry: Understanding Prison Culture Inside and Out* (Nashville, TN: B & H Publishing Group, 2002), p. 196.

9. These commitments may be found in Awana Lifeline materials available at www.awanalifeline.org.

10. Donald Braman, *Doing Time on the Outside: Incarceration and Family Life in Urban America* (Ann Arbor: University of Michigan Press, 2009), p.10.

11. Ibid, p. 90.

12. Conversation with Dr. Kristi Miller, Louisiana State Prison for Women, February 6, 2014.

13. Returning Hearts is a ministry strategy of Awana Lifeline. It is a celebration where inmates and their children can unite for a day of games, food, relationship building, biblical teaching, and possibly reconciliation.

14. Topics are gleaned from a series entitled *Transforming Dads Incarcerated* (Aurora, IL: New Life Corrections Ministry, Wayside Cross Ministries, Tom Beatty, director, n.d.).

15. Catherine Stonehouse, "Conversation," *Evangelical Dictionary of Christian Education* edited by Michael J. Anthony (Grand Rapids, MI: Baker Academic, 2001), p. 176.

16. *How to Teach Kids Using Guided Conversation (Grades 1-6)* (Ventura, CA: Gospel Light, 1993), p. 3.

17. Julie A. Gorman, *Community That Is Christian: A Handbook on Small Groups*, 2nd Edition (Grand Rapids, MI: Baker Books, 2002), p. 98.

18. Bill Donahue, *Leading Life-Changing Small Groups* (Grand Rapids, MI: Zondervan, 2002), p. 118.

[19] Timothy Keller, *Center Church: Doing Balanced, Gospel-Centered Ministry in Your City* (Grand Rapids, MI: Zondervan, 2012), p. 75.

[20] Dave Arch, *Creative Training Techniques 1* (Minneapolis: The Bob Pike Group, 2000), pp. 14-15.

[21] Clarence H. Benson, *Biblical Beliefs: Doctrines Believers Should Know* (Wheaton, IL: Evangelical Training Association, 2001) pp. 5-6.

Chapter 4

INVITATION TO A PRISON GUARD

*Then he brought them out and said,
"Sirs, what must I do to be saved?"
And they said, "Believe in the Lord Jesus,
and you will be saved, you and
your household."*

Acts 16:30-31

Memory Verses

KEY VERSES

Invitation to a Prison Guard

Then he brought them out and said, "Sirs, what must I do to be saved?" And they said, "Believe in the Lord Jesus, and you will be saved, you and your household." (Acts 16:30-31)

CHALLENGE VERSES 1

Summary of the Gospel

For I delivered to you as of first importance what I also received: that Christ died for our sins in accordance with the Scriptures, that He was buried, that He was raised on the third day in accordance with the Scriptures, and that He appeared to Cephas, then to the twelve. (1 Corinthians 15:3-5)

CHALLENGE VERSE 2

Power of the Gospel

For I am not ashamed of the gospel, for it is the power of God for salvation to everyone who believes, to the Jew first and also to the Greek. (Romans 1:16)

Gospel of Grace

BIG IDEA

The gospel of grace is the power of God to change a person's life. Clearly and confidently sharing the message of truth is the joy and witness of the facilitator in prison ministry. **What must I do to be saved?** is the salvation question.

FOUNDATION

The gospel is the foundation of our ministry to prisoners. We must be clear and faithful in our presentation. To be so, we need to first ground ourselves in the purity and simplicity of the gospel. What is the gospel?

Gospel simply means "good news." The Bible uses the term to refer to the message that God has fulfilled His promise to send a Savior to rescue broken people, restore creation's glory, and rule over all with compassion and justice. That's why a good summary of the gospel is *... Christ Jesus came into the world to save sinners ... (1 Timothy 1:15).*

> Gospel means "good news."

Parrett and Kang quote J. I. Packer as summing up the gospel in three words: "God saves sinners."[1]

Some might dismiss the discussion of the gospel and salvation as a theological exercise that has little impact on real ministry. But what you believe impacts how you behave! If you believe that the gospel is the power of God to change a life, then your actions of proclaiming salvation through Christ alone have meaning. If you do not understand the gospel, there is the potential to proclaim a distorted message, even as there was in Paul's day: *I am astonished that you are so quickly deserting Him who called you in the grace of Christ and are turning to a different gospel — not that there is another one, but there are some who trouble you and want to distort the gospel of Christ (Galatians 1:6-7).*

> What you believe impacts how you behave!

After hearing an inspiring song being sung at a church in the Midwest, a seminary professor proclaimed, "I just got saved!" Disbelief and amazement abounded as the congregation pondered that an evangelical leader would just at that moment get saved! The problem, of course, resides in differing definitions of salvation and what aspect is being described!

Justification — being *saved* from the penalty of sin

Sanctification — being *saved* from the power of sin

Glorification — being *saved* from the presence of sin

These three are all facets of a full biblical definition of salvation. Misunderstandings and frustration can occur when Scriptures about sanctification are employed to describe justification. We actually diminish the gospel of grace and change it into a system of works! Likewise, confusion about the difference between our regeneration experience (justification) and spending eternity with Christ (glorification) may occur. "Although a believer can never lose his justification salvation, there are dimensions of glorification salvation that may be lost or gained if we take seriously passages such as Romans 14:10, 1 Corinthians 3:15, 2 Corinthians 5:10, and 2 John 7-8."[2]

The gospel provides salvation!

Salvation That Day — Justification

The topic of salvation as justification could have entire books written about it (and has)! In a culture which thrives on cause and effect, salvation by grace through faith is missed in two ways. One, we have difficulty believing that we don't need to earn our standing with God. Second, we too often diminish the reality of sin in our lives and the price that Christ paid on the cross. Paul confronted Peter with the simplicity of the gospel: *Yet we know that a person is not justified by works of the law but through faith in Jesus Christ, so we also have believed in Christ Jesus, in order to be justified by faith in Christ and not by works of the law, because by works of the law no one will be justified (Galatians 2:16).*

Salvation that day
– justification

Four themes clarify the gospel of grace in salvation (justification).

Grace — "Amazing grace! How sweet the sound, That saved a wretch like me!" The old gospel hymn reveals a wondrous truth: God reached down to the sinner (you and me!) while we were still hostile toward Him, and paid the price to give us the free gift of life in Christ. "Grace is an outrage ... Our merit-based economics and resumé-building selves don't sit well with unmerited favor."[3] When we say the gospel of grace, it is to assure that we did not seek for our salvation in the first place, we did not pay for our salvation, and we certainly did not earn or work for our salvation. Billy Graham said, "Grace is not sought nor bought nor wrought, it is a free gift of Almighty God to needy mankind."[4]

"Grace is not sought nor bought nor wrought."

Faith — The key verse for this chapter happened within a prison context. Thinking the prisoners in his care had escaped, the jailor was about to take his own life. Paul and Silas prevented him from doing so, and directed him to believe in the Lord Jesus Christ for his salvation (Acts 16:30-31).

Faith exhibits itself when a person believes — trusts, relies upon, rests in — the person and work of Christ. *For by grace you have been saved through faith. And this is not your own doing; it is the gift of God, not a result of works, so that no one may boast (Ephesians 2:8-9).* Faith is "a firm conviction, producing a full acknowledgement of God's revelation or truth, e.g., 2 Thessalonians 2:11-12; a personal surrender to Him, John 1:12; and a conduct inspired by such surrender, 2 Corinthians 5:7."[5]

Repentance is often associated with and accompanying faith. "To turn to Christ, looking to Him for deliverance, hope, and life is to also turn away from self and all other rival kings. Trusting in Christ requires turning from sin."[6]

Sin — Teaching about and exposing the meaning and depth of sin is difficult in a culture of secret (Ephesians 5:12), evil behavior, and suppressing truth (Romans 1:19). Modern politicians, philosophers, scientists, psychologists, and sociologists often propose remedies for the ills of our world. But remedies that don't take into account this understanding of sin are mere child's play because they have not begun to understand the depth of the human predicament. Humans can't solve their deep, universal problem of sin. Only God can.[7]

Sin's wages are death (Romans 6:23) and transgressions' impact is to separate us from experiencing a relationship with a holy God: *Behold, the LORD's hand is not shortened, that it cannot save, or His ear dull, that it cannot hear; but your iniquities have made a separation between you and your God, and your sins have hidden His face from you so that He does not hear (Isaiah 59:1-2).* We need a Savior! "God created us to have a relationship with us. But first the bad news: Sin has separated us from God, and no amount of goodness on our part can bridge the chasm between us and God."[8]

Cross — An instrument of capital punishment (the cross) has become a symbol of life and beauty! We put the cross on our church buildings and wear it as jewelry. The cross of Calvary should be more than decoration, it should be the focal point of a person's faith. Wuest summarizes and exhorts in relation to the cross: "Dear reader, if you have been depending in the least upon any personal merit, will you not now cast aside all this, and accept the free grace of God by faith in Jesus Christ as your personal Savior, the One who died on the cross for you, pouring out His precious blood as the God-appointed sacrifice for sins?"[9]

The salvation that is justification results in a life of faith.

Salvation Today — Sanctification

Salvation as sanctification is expressed by the apostle Paul in his letter to the church in Philippi. *Therefore, my beloved, as you have always obeyed, so now, not only as in my presence but much more in my absence, work out your own salvation with fear and trembling, for it is God who works in you, both to will and to work for His good pleasure (Philippians 2:12-13).* One Bible teacher we had in college often said, "You have to *work out* what God has *worked in*!" Sanctification is the process of becoming like Jesus Christ in every aspect of how we live. Theologian Michael Bird calls this the "'drama of *gospelizing*' which is 'trying to become what the gospel intends believers to be: slaves of Christ, vessels of grace, agents of the kingdom, and a people worthy of God's name.'"[10]

> Salvation today — sanctification

Doubt about the genuineness of the faith of inmates' conversion is certainly a legitimate issue. Observations about a get out of jail free mentality abound, as if the gospel ministry is a Monopoly® game. "When hearing of the reality of Christian inmates, some will ask, almost with incredulity, 'But, do you think they've *really* changed?'"[11] Perhaps the spectrum of persistence in the Christian life for those incarcerated is very much like the response with anyone. And that's the

> "You have to *work out* what God has *worked in*!"

problem. We don't want to face the thought that a person who says they have believed in Christ doesn't seem to grow in Christ. Pastor and speaker Francis Chan addresses this issue: "I'm not saying that when you mess up, it means you were never really a genuine Christian in the first place. If that were true, no one could follow Christ. The distinction is perfection (which none will attain on this earth) and a posture of obedience and surrender, where a person perpetually moves toward Christ."[12]

We should expect the life of Christ to be increasing in the life of the believer, whether in prison or on the outside. Jesus complimented Zacchaeus on the life change that occurred: *And Jesus said to him, "Today salvation has come to this house, since he also is a son of Abraham" (Luke 19:9).* Salvation didn't come to the tax collector because he made restitution; restitution was made because salvation had come to him. It was a sanctification moment — a setting apart from sin and to God.

W. E. Vine defines sanctification in the New Testament as having two basic understandings. One is the relationship with God where the believer is set apart in that relationship by the merits of Christ. This definition is the sanctification that happens when a believer is justified and regenerated. Sanctification also occurs as: "The separation of the believer from evil things and ways. This sanctification is God's will for the believer, and His purpose in calling him by the gospel; it must be learned from God, as He teaches it by His Word; and it must be pursued by the believer, earnestly and undeviatingly. For the holy character … cannot be transferred or imputed, it is an individual possession, built up, little by little, as the result of obedience to the Word of God, and of following the example of Christ, in the power of the Holy Spirit."[13] (Bible references deleted.)

Sanctification — holy living — should be expected, sought, taught, pursued, and unhindered. It cannot be done on one's own, it must be a process of faith: *Therefore, as you received Christ Jesus the Lord, so walk in Him (Colossians 2:6).*

The lack of sanctification is especially troubling when it describes a member of your own family. Therefore, the sanctifying work of the Holy Spirit becomes also the basis of trust in reestablishing relationships with children and/or spouse.

The importance of an inmate having his/her heart changed by the gospel cannot be over-emphasized. In discussing the post-prison rehabilitation of black inmates, Marvin Williams states: "Rehabilitation began with Jesus Christ and Him changing their (inmates') hearts. This is the most important theological issue upon which the church can begin to build a rehabilitative system for offenders and ex-offenders."[14]

The salvation that is sanctification results in a life of love.

Salvation Someday — Glorification

Heaven and hell, eternal life, and eternal death are common themes in presenting the gospel. Salvation does have a future for the believer. One inmate described his life as a living hell! This thought crossed our minds: If you only knew! Hell is even more serious than this! Heaven is not just a concept of comfort for people whose life is miserable now. Heaven is a reality. In times past, evangelism focused much upon where you will be when you die! We both came to believe in Christ as our Savior after hearing talk about the terribleness of hell! Discussion of where a person spends eternity is appropriate because of their current belief. Randy Newman shares of people responding to death in four ways:

1. They fear it with horror.
2. They ignore it in denial.
3. They cling to false hope.
4. They overcome it in the gospel.

Salvation someday — glorification

Our task in evangelism centers on contrasting the first three responses to the fourth. The distinct nature of the finished work of the gospel delivers people from fear, denial, or false hope.[15]

Eternal life with God is motivation to share the gospel: *Therefore I endure everything for the sake of the elect, that they also may obtain the salvation that is in Christ Jesus with eternal glory (2 Timothy 2:10).* When a prisoner dies, or when someone is on death row, the seriousness of faith is accentuated. The infusion of hope through the gospel of Christ allows a facilitator to assure the believer of a future in heaven, those *who by God's power are being guarded through faith for a salvation ready to be revealed in the last time (1 Peter 1:5).*

The resurrection of Jesus Christ is the basis of our future hope. Hope! That's what our future holds. Paul wrote to the Thessalonian church about the steadfastness of hope (1 Thessalonians 1:3) that caused them to become a proclaiming people (1 Thessalonians 1:8) and a church that looked forward to the day when Jesus would return. He describes the believers' behavior: *And to wait for His Son from heaven, whom He raised from the dead, Jesus who delivers us from the wrath to come (1 Thessalonians 1:10).* "If those of us who are Christian educators and ministers to those in the emerging generations of the church fail to emphasize the centrality of the resurrection event, we are failing to give our Christian young people a full, biblical understanding of our salvation, which comes through Jesus Christ. The resurrection guarantees our future resurrection and eternal life with God."[16]

Teaching about the resurrection of Christ extends this hope for incarcerated people. Because He lives, we will live with Him eternally.

The salvation that is glorification results in a life of hope.

PRINCIPLES

Three principles guide the application of the gospel of grace to life and ministry.

Present the Gospel

Share the gospel — Returning to our high school alma mater for homecoming, we as peers were comparing notes about being away from our hometown. A fellow classmate shared of his becoming a Christian his first year of college. While a couple of us were congratulating him on his new faith, hoping to encourage him, he abruptly directed his look and thoughts saying, "You never told me!" He explained the fun and study together during school days had almost always tipped him off to a difference between us, but it took a university student Bible study leader to actually tell him about the gospel. Prayers for him, invitations to him, living in faith in front of him still lacked the words to help him understand the gospel. We are not called to mime the gospel, we are called to tell it!

Seize the opportunities — Evangelist Mark Cahill states, "I firmly believe that we must change our mindset about sharing our faith. We must view it as the awesome opportunity that it is and not as some sort of drudgery."[17] Prison ministry is not immune from some of the same fears that hold us back from presenting the gospel anywhere else. Even when we are motivated to participate in leading inmates in small-group study, we can find ourselves reluctant to share our faith. Presenting the gospel is focusing on "the infectious nature of God's heart and tapping into His plan for using His Spirit in the believer to draw the lost to Himself. It's also about rediscovering the joy of our salvation and wanting to see that joy in others."[18]

Participate in the Gospel

Showing Christ — To participate in the gospel is not just to have a faith for oneself. It means to also live out publicly the character of Christ. Life change is expected! "Lukewarm living and claiming Christ's name simultaneously is utterly disgusting to God … God wants to change us; He died so that we could change. The answer lies in letting Him change you … Jesus Christ didn't die only to save us from hell; He also died to save us from our bondage to sin."[19]

To model what it means to know Christ in faithfulness is also essential. Paul urges Titus to teach a sound doctrine lifestyle so *… that the word of God may not be reviled (Titus 2:5).* Hypocrisy is a very real hindrance to people's faith. A young woman struggled with believing in Christ, and frankly, had acted out in sinful and destructive ways. She blamed her father's hypocrisy for her troubles — a man who abused her and also served as a deacon in his church.

Sticky Faith — Sticky faith is the term Powell, Griffin, and Crawford coined to describe a faith that persists, even after a Christian student goes to college. Prison ministry has the same concern but in a different arena: when the incarcerated person is released. Our aim is to have faith that lasts, whether an adolescent heading off to college or an inmate going home. Sticky faith is:

Sticky Faith

---

1. Both internal and external: Sticky faith is part of a student's (prisoner's) inner thoughts and emotions, and is also externalized in choices and actions that reflect this faith commitment …

2. Both personal and communal: Sticky faith celebrates God's specific care for each person while always locating faith in the global and local community of the church.

3. Both mature and maturing: Sticky faith shows marks of spiritual maturity but is also in the process of growth.[20]

Prepare Others in the Gospel

Helping others as they learn to share their faith is discipleship at work. While prison ministry is a fertile field of endeavor, it does have its difficult cultivations. It is hard work at times. *Therefore I endure everything for the sake of the elect, that they also may*

*obtain the salvation that is in Christ Jesus with eternal glory
(2 Timothy 2:10).* The younger generations are increasingly illiterate about the fundamentals of the gospel. "In our American culture, one can no longer assume even a rudimentary acquaintance with the Bible or the claims of Christ. Many young people coming into prison today have never even heard that Jesus died on the cross for their sins."[21]

On the other hand, a great hunger can be in the life of an incarcerated person. The responsiveness of those who have been impacted by crime is often magnified. Lampman and Shattuck describe three responses to a victim's spiritual needs. 1. Faith that heals — "faith deepened and strengthened as a result of the crisis." 2. Faith that questions — "putting faith to a severe test." 3. Faith that seeks — "For some victims, crime touches a spiritual chord that has long been silent or has never been played."[22]

Preparing the inmates to serve others in their small group, their sphere of influence in the prison, and their own families is essential. Timothy Keller describes renewal of the gospel in the local church "through the training of lay leaders who minister the gospel to others."[23] We want to raise up parents, incarcerated or not, who are able to teach the truth of the gospel, present and persuade with care, and provide a place where others are able to believe in Jesus Christ as their Savior.

METHOD: EVANGELISM

Three features of training others in the gospel comprise what we call evangelism training: the message (content of the good news, partially described above in the Foundation Section), the messenger (couriers are the believers who are motivated to live and share the message), and the means (connections of overcoming barriers, both personally and in the inmate).

Content of the Gospel — The gospel doesn't change, because God has established it. However, the way we share the gospel adapts to our present culture. "Christians should acknowledge the role that context plays in anyone's understanding and belief. 'Truth' is always held by actual persons, and those persons are deeply shaped by culture, language, heritage, and community."[24]

Message – content of the gospel

A group of children's and youth ministry experts were discussing how to share the message of the gospel of grace with young people. It was determined that we could portray the facets of the gospel in what came to be called The Gospel Wheel.[25] This tool has been effective in allowing a flexible yet biblical means of sharing the message of the good news.

The unchanging tenets of the gospel were described in the Foundation Section above. Creative, Scriptural ways to present the gospel to inmates are always appropriate.

Couriers of the Gospel — Promptings for the messenger's motivation — Believers are called to share the good news of life in Christ. Paul shared his motivations for sharing the gospel, and we do well to consider them for ourselves:

• The fear of the Lord — *Therefore, knowing the fear of the Lord, we persuade others … (2 Corinthians 5:11)*

• The love of Christ — *For the love of Christ controls us, because we have concluded this: that one has died for all, therefore all have died. (2 Corinthians 5:14)*

Messenger – courier of the gospel

• Necessity or responsibility — *For if I preach the gospel, that gives me no ground for boasting. For necessity is laid upon me. Woe to me if I do not preach the gospel! (1 Corinthians 9:16)*

Connections for the Gospel —

- Prayer — We must connect with God in prayer before we connect with people in evangelism. "The key practice that distinguishes evangelism-fruitful student leaders from others is their pattern of prayer."[26]

Means – connections for the gospel

- People — Learning to have compassion for the prisoner (or any other person outside of Christ) is the pathway of effectiveness. "My prayer is that … you will find renewed joy in loving the non-Christian, that you will be granted freedom to wait for God's timing, and that you will become addicted to sharing the message of grace."[27]

- Process — Evangelism Explosion has effectively trained people to share the gospel for decades. They employ three types of training: class instruction, homework assignments, and on-the-job. In being effective in leading others to Christ, we should look for mentors who will do evangelism with us and not just expect us to be able to do this on our own.

ORAL METHOD: PICTURES AND VISUALS

We encounter the power of pictures and visuals whether in newspaper or magazine print, billboard advertising, or comic reading. Your adaptability in the use of these illustrations will not only highlight the message of the gospel but also assist the one who struggles with identifying, understanding, or comprehending the words. The examples of easy stick-figure drawings or elaborate pictures, drawn by hand or published in color, spontaneous or planned, can enhance your teaching. Following are several approaches in which the gospel has been shared in prison ministry, even when the one who is hearing cannot read well.

Gospel Wheel — Described above and in Appendix A.

Bridge to Life — "This popular little booklet from The Navigators® presents the gospel clearly, using simple diagrams and selected Scriptures to explain the need for salvation and how to come to faith in Christ."[28]

Three Simple Truths — With a bucket, container, bowl or glass Kristi Miller uses this visual word picture to share the gospel creatively.

TEACHING POINTERS

Teach centering on the gospel of grace. The emphasis is repeated again because it is often easy to become distracted from the core of our faith — believing the gospel! Even as we use Bible-based curriculum, we must give attention ourselves to focus on presenting the message of salvation. Theologians Carson and Keller convey this importance as they describe the purpose of the Gospel Coalition: "We believe that some important aspects of the historic understanding of the biblical gospel are in danger of being muddied or lost in our churches today. These include the necessity of the new birth, justification by faith alone, and atonement through propitiation and the substitutionary death of Christ."[29]

These doctrines may seem too weighty for the usual facilitator. However, knowing the meaning of these doctrines will give confidence in teaching effectively.

Teach all within the prison sphere of influence. We are speaking, of course, about prison officers. The apostle Paul reported that his imprisonment was an advance for the gospel and that the whole imperial guard had heard the good news (Philippians 1:12- 13). He may have played a good part in that! Being chained or watching over the apostolic prisoner for rotating shifts might have exposed the officers to the message Paul preached. We should be mindful of prison officials, those in direct responsibility and with authority, who need to hear the gospel also. "May the opportunities continue for Christians to share, sensitively but clearly, the Lord Jesus Christ with prison officers!"[30]

Teach for forgiveness. Forgiveness is very important to teach in prison ministry. To forgive themselves is the first step for inmates. A few continue to blame the justice system or others they feel are responsible. Some are even bold enough to acknowledge their difficulty in believing God could forgive them. Mike Broyles, executive director of Awana Lifeline, considers this topic to be of great importance and makes it a priority to review it with the inmate dads or moms before every Returning Hearts Celebration.

Notes

1   Gary A. Parrett and S. Steve Kang, *Teaching the Faith, Forming the Faithful* (Downers Grove, IL: IVP Academic, 2009), p. 103.

2   Earl D. Radmacher, in Jody Dillow, *The Reign of the Servant Kings* (Hayesville, NC: Schoettle Publishing Co., 1992), p. xiii.

3   Randy Newman, *Bringing the Gospel Home: Witnessing to Family Members, Close Friends, and Others Who Know You Well* (Wheaton, IL: Crossway, 2011), p. 59.

4   As quoted in Wayne A. Detzler, *New Testament Words in Today's Language* (Wheaton, IL: Victor Books, 1986), p. 189.

5   W. E. Vine, *An Expository Dictionary of New Testament Words* (Old Tappan, NJ: Fleming H. Revell Company, 1940, 1966), Vol. II, p. 71.

6   W. Jackson Watts, *Biblical Beliefs: Doctrines Believers Should Know* (Wheaton, IL: Evangelical Training Association, 2013), p. 76.

7   Reddit Andrews III, "Sin and the Fall," in *The Gospel as Center: Renewing Our Faith and Reforming Our Ministry Practices* edited by Timothy Keller and D. A. Carson (Wheaton, IL: The Gospel Coalition, Crossway, 2012), p. 86.

8   Kevin Riggs, *Evangelism for the 21st Century* (Wheaton, IL: Evangelical Training Association, 2014), p. 11.

9   Kenneth S. Wuest, "Ephesians and Colossians in the Greek New Testament," *Wuest's Word Studies From the Greek New Testament* (Grand Rapids, MI: Wm. B. Eerdmans Publishing Company, 1953), pp. 23-24.

10   Michael S. Bird, *Evangelical Theology* (Grand Rapids, MI: Zondervan, 2013), p. 30.

11   Lennie Spitale, *Prison Ministry: Understanding Prison Culture Inside and Out* (Nashville, TN: B & H Publishing Group, 2002), p. 6.

12   Francis Chan, *Crazy Love: Overwhelmed by a Relentless God* (Colorado Springs: David C. Cook, 2008), p. 88.

13   Vine, *An Expository Dictionary of New Testament Words*, Vol. III, p. 317.

14   Marvin L. Williams, *Beyond the Bars: The Black Church and Its Responsibility in Prison/Aftercare Ministry* (Unpublished thesis, Trinity Evangelical Divinity School, 1993), p. 104.

15   Newman, *Bringing the Gospel Home: Witnessing to Family Members, Close Friends, and Others Who Know You Well,* pp. 181-182.

16   Jason Carlson, "Jesus: Risen for a New Generation," in *Apologetics for a New Generation,* general editor Sean McDowell (Eugene, OR: Harvest House Publishers, 2009), p. 183.

17   Mark Cahill, *One Thing You Can't Do in Heaven* (Rockwall, TX: Biblical Discipleship Ministries, 2004), p. 22.

18   Michael L. Simpson, *Permission Evangelism: When to Talk, When to Walk* (Colorado Springs: Cook Communications Ministries, 2003), p. 10.

[19] Chan, *Crazy Love*, p. 103.

[20] Kara E. Powell, Brad M. Griffin, and Cheryl A. Crawford, *Sticky Faith* (Grand Rapids, MI: Zondervan, 2011), p. 21.

[21] Spitale, Prison Ministry: *Understanding Prison Culture Inside and Out*, p. 195.

[22] Lisa Barnes Lampman and Michelle D. Shattuck, "Finding God in the Wake of Crime: Answers to Hard Questions," in *God and the Victim* edited by Lisa Barnes Lampman and Michelle D. Shattuck (Grand Rapids, MI: William B. Eerdmans Publishing Co., 1999), pp. 9-10, 12.

[23] Timothy Keller, *Center Church: Doing Balanced, Gospel-Centered Ministry in Your City* (Grand Rapids, MI: Zondervan, 2012), p. 74.

[24] Richard D. Phillips, "Can We Know the Truth?" in *The Gospel as Center: Renewing Our Faith and Reforming Our Ministry Practices* edited by Timothy Keller and D. A. Carson (Wheaton, IL: The Gospel Coalition, Crossway, 2012), p. 25.

[25] The Gospel Wheel is a visual means of sharing the gospel using Scripture. It is available in Appendix A of this book and online as the Awana Gospel Message App.

[26] Dave Rahn and Terry Linhart, *Contagious Faith* (Loveland, CO: Group Publishing, 2000), p. 57.

[27] Michael L. Simpson, *Permission Evangelism: When to Talk, When to Walk*, p. 11.

[28] Navigators, *Bridge to Life* (Colorado Springs: NavPress, 2007).

[29] D. A. Carson and Timothy Keller, "Gospel-Centered Ministry," in *The Gospel as Center: Renewing Our Faith and Reforming Our Ministry Practices* edited by Timothy Keller and D. A. Carson (Wheaton, IL: The Gospel Coalition, Crossway, 2012), p. 11.

[30] Gerard Crispin, *Beyond Bars: Looking Inside the Inside Story* (Ryelands Road, Leominster, UK: Day One Publications, 2007), p. 66.

KEY VERSES

Chapter 5

MINISTRY OF MATURITY/CHRISTLIKENESS

*Him we proclaim, warning everyone
and teaching everyone with all wisdom,
that we may present everyone mature
in Christ. For this I toil, struggling
with all His energy that He
powerfully works within me.*

Colossians 1:28-29

Memory Verses

KEY VERSES

Ministry of Maturity/Christlikeness

Him we proclaim, warning everyone and teaching everyone with all wisdom, that we may present everyone mature in Christ. For this I toil, struggling with all His energy that He powerfully works within me. (Colossians 1:28-29)

CHALLENGE VERSES 1

Paul's Testimony

And now, behold, I am going to Jerusalem, constrained by the Spirit, not knowing what will happen to me there, except that the Holy Spirit testifies to me in every city that imprisonment and afflictions await me. But I do not account my life of any value nor as precious to myself, if only I may finish my course and the ministry that I received from the Lord Jesus, to testify to the gospel of the grace of God. (Acts 20:22-24)

CHALLENGE VERSES 2

Exhortations for Leaders

And we urge you, brothers, admonish the idle, encourage the fainthearted, help the weak, be patient with them all. See that no one repays anyone evil for evil, but always seek to do good to one another and to everyone. Rejoice always, pray without ceasing. (1 Thessalonians 5:14-17)

Guide for Life Change

BIG IDEA

Being prepared for prison ministry in knowledge, attitude, and skills is the goal of the servant of Christ. Serving the Lord and leading those entrusted to my care fulfills the call to ministry. **How do I do this?** is the operational question.

FOUNDATION

The Scriptures give us the answers to the operational question of How do I do this?

Complete in Christ, Colossians 1:27-29

• Proclamation — ... *Christ in you, the hope of glory (Colossians 1:27)* is "the amazing hallmark of the new covenant ... God Himself, in the person of Christ, will be directly and personally present in the lives of His people."[1] This is the powerful and life-changing message that is proclaimed in the ministry described by Paul in the book of Colossians. It was stated to refute false teachers, who

> Christ in you, the hope of glory

were persuading people of a secret perfection that came above and beyond the gospel of Christ. Christ in the believer is the message that counterbalances this error, both in the Colossian church and in the prison where you serve.

To *proclaim* is to "announce, far and wide"[2], "not a system of doctrine so much as a Person, the Lord Jesus."[3] As we are involved in prison ministry, it is well to remember this! We go to announce and invite others to know the person of the Lord Jesus Christ, not a doctrinal system only about Him. A relationship with Christ is our hope, not a series of studies, as helpful as they may be.

- Warning – Warning could also be translated as admonishing or counseling. Our ministry should mirror this dimension of urgent alerting and counsel. In Paul's day, some wanted to reach only Jewish individuals with the gospel. In our day, we want to influence every race and condition of people.

- Teaching – We have defined teaching as "One hand on the Word of God, the other on the student, bringing them together for life change." If we are to teach with this approach, we will need to know the Bible (Chapter 2), know the students (Chapter 3), and seek to set an environment where the Holy Spirit will change their lives (Chapter 4, the gospel, and Chapter 5, guide for life change). To know and interpret the Scriptures is essential. To study and understand the students we teach is vital. Trusting the Holy Spirit to change the hearts and lives of the ones we teach is the priority.

> Be creative and wise in *how* we teach as in *what* we teach.

We are to teach *with all wisdom*. Awareness of Jesus being the full revelation of God's wisdom (Ephesians 3:10) means more than just an agreement with doctrine. We share in that wisdom. It means we are training in the life of Christ presently (sanctification) and will enjoy glorification in Christ in eternity (2 Thessalonians 2:14, Romans 8:30). However, many who are wise in Christ are foolish in teaching methodology. They know splendor in belief, but are boring in their practice of teaching, which is the purpose of the Teaching Pointers at the end of each chapter. It is our hope we would be creative and wise in *how* we teach as in *what* we teach.

- Completeness – Maturity in Christ is the goal and motivation for ministry. To be mature is to be complete or perfect (both words are used interchangeably with maturity in the Bible). We could illustrate this concept by asking the question, "What are the *ingredients* of a *perfect* cookie?" Our usual list would be composed, with the careful inclusion of chocolate chips. We would then discuss the process of *making* the cookie, including baking. Finally, we would anticipate the *full participation* in not only smelling the cookie but also enjoying its taste. Three lessons emerge from the making of a perfect cookie:

1. The Holy Spirit uses our ministry to guarantee *no part is missing!* We warn all about what is lacking in their practice or behavior. We teach about proper doctrine or belief.

2. The Holy Spirit guides the process of growth to ensure we are *not half-baked!* Often inmates will make an initial statement of faith and take establishing steps. But soon, the Evil One places doubt in their minds and sluggishness in their behaviors. They can fall short of maturity. Paul outlines the Lord's work in the lives of the Colossians: *And you, who once were alienated and hostile in mind, doing evil deeds, He has now reconciled in His body of flesh by His death, in order to present you holy and blameless and above reproach before Him, if indeed you continue in the faith, stable and steadfast, not shifting from the hope of the gospel that you heard, which has been proclaimed in all creation under heaven, and of which I, Paul, became a minister (Colossians 1:21-23).*

3. The Holy Spirit promotes abundance in and through the life of the believer — *there's plenty to go around!* We should expect a ministry where people come to know Christ as their Savior, but we don't stop with that! We encourage a moving toward maturity (Philippians 3:12-14) and reproducing in another spiritual generation (Hebrews 5:11-14).

- Hard Work – Too many expect when they begin serving the Lord that life should be easy. They are ambushed by the amount of hours and effort ministry sometimes takes. The Holy Spirit will also supply strength and energy for this ministry.

Constrained by the Holy Spirit, Acts 20:22-24

Lessons on the Holy Spirit's enabling in ministry have previously been mentioned. However, by studying Paul's summary of his ministry in Acts 20, we are able to glean other principles to guide us in our own service.

- The future need not concern us. Paul faced this reality in his own life: *... not knowing what will happen to me there (Acts 20:22).* Uncertainties of timing, place, and influences did not devastate Paul. For many incarcerated parents, concern for their families is overwhelming. Hope of getting out of prison as soon as possible and resuming normal family living seem almost all-encompassing. Others fear the future, particularly if they are facing a long or life sentence or are on death row. Prison ministry expert Lennie Spitale reminds us of our greatest potential for ministry: "Let them know that this One who holds the future in His hands desires that they should share their futures with Him. It is not our job to cause inmates to put their hopes in their release dates. If that were the case, what would our ministry to lifers be? It is not our job to predict that God will prepare them for a great work on the outside someday (though for some that may well be the case), but to let them know that no day is ever wasted in His sight and that He has a purpose for them right where they are. Nor is it our job to say that God will give them the peace they need to make it only to their release dates, but that God has true and lasting peace available to every one of His children right now, no matter what their circumstances. There is another day coming. Another time coming. One that, if they are Christians, can never be feared because its joys can never end."[4]

- Difficulties should not surprise us. We often pray (as we should) that the logistical details of ministry not hinder us. Security issues, timing, absences of leaders or inmates, and other concerns can discourage us. Some of these obstacles cannot be overcome by hard work because their source is in a higher, invisible realm: *For we do not wrestle against flesh and blood, but against the rulers, against the authorities, against the cosmic powers over this present darkness, against the spiritual forces of evil in the heavenly places (Ephesians 6:12).*

While traveling in western Ukraine, a conversation with the pastor involved in a prison ministry in Dragovich gave us insights about the desperate conditions of some of the prisoners, the lack of resources to minister to their needs, and the too-few volunteers from his church. He was greatly encouraged, though, because in the midst of all these difficulties, men were being changed by the gospel!

- A proper view of ourselves releases us. Paul testified: *But I do not account my life of any value nor as precious to myself, if only I may finish my course and the ministry that I received from the Lord Jesus ... (Acts 20:24).* We have found that we can be intimidated when facing new situations, especially ones that are not pleasant or expected. It is at those times that faith is most needed. Trusting the One who called us, who knows us better than we know ourselves, is the turning point of victory!

- The owner of ministry empowers us. Jesus Christ has called us; His is the ministry given to us! When an inmate is transformed by the gospel, it is not unusual to see a zeal for ministry that surpasses those of us who live on the outside. Freedom, finances, and family support may be stripped but the Lord Jesus is still with them. Paul had a similar attitude of dependency for his ministry. He asked who is adequate or sufficient for the ministry (2 Corinthians 2:16). Paul found his confidence to be in the grace and power the Lord gave (2 Corinthians 3:4-6).

- The gospel is proclaimed through us. In all of this the priority of presenting the gospel is maintained. Paul seemed to be addicted to presenting the gospel. *So I am eager to preach the gospel to you also who are in Rome. For I am not ashamed of the gospel, for it is the power of God for salvation to everyone who believes … (Romans 1:15-16).* We should have similar passion.

PRINCIPLES

If you are reading this, we assume you have a Holy Spirit constraining to involve yourself in prison ministry (Acts 20:22). This sense of being drawn to the ministry may have been brewing over a period of time, be recent in your awareness, or be integral in your ministry lifestyle. If this chapter is the first chapter you have read, we strongly suggest, though, you read the first four chapters. Their intent is to give you depth in leading the ministry to which you are called. If you have been applying the material as you have read, we hope by now that you are ready to bolster your confidence and polish your skills.

Preparation for This Ministry

How should facilitators for a prison ministry prepare themselves? What attitudes should be developed and groomed for maximum ministry? In our work with young adults, we often are asked, "What do you think God's will is for my life and future ministry?" The answers we give to these young leaders just starting out in a lifetime of service may also set the parameters for volunteer guides of prison Bible studies. In the New Testament at least six times, the clear statement of God's will is expressed. What is God's will for you?

Maturing and Spirit-filled — To be mature takes time. To be filled with the Spirit can happen today. When we are filled with the Spirit, we begin to mature and we are able to take advantage of every opportunity. The verses in Ephesians 5:15-16 speak of the days being evil and making the best use of time. They are followed by a command to be filled with the Spirit in Ephesians 5:17-18. Being filled with the Spirit is like spiritual breathing for the believer.

God's will is accomplished as we yield to the Holy Spirit. The power to live the Christian life comes by being rightly related to the Spirit. It should be noted that one of the first signs of being filled with the Holy Spirit is a proper relationship within the family (Ephesians 5:22-6:4). A marriage relationship can be compared to the mystery of Christ and the Church (Ephesians 5:32) and parenting demonstrates *the discipline and instruction of the Lord (Ephesians 6:4)*. These are normal, expected outcomes of being a person who walks in the Spirit.

Sincere and Serving — As a guide begins to work with incarcerated people, it might be tempting to think of the service as being for the good of the inmate, the benefit of the ministry, or for personal satisfaction. All of these have their place, but the priority and passion of serving in this ministry is *not by the way of eye-service, as people-pleasers, but as bondservants of Christ, doing the will of God from the heart, rendering service with a good will as to the Lord and not to man (Ephesians 6:6-7)*.

Wise and Pure — In praying with a group of young men who were involved in a Bible-teaching project together, one prayed, "Lord, don't let me do anything that would embarrass You!" That may very well be our attitude as we go into the small group. 1 Thessalonians 4:1-7 states that it is God's will for us to be practicing sanctification, especially in the area of sexual purity. Too many ministries have been hindered or destroyed in our supercharged, sensuality-driven culture by careless disregard for proper conduct in this area. We should seek to model sound intergenerational relationships: *Do not rebuke an older man but encourage him as you would a father, younger men as brothers, older women as mothers, younger women as sisters, in all purity (1 Timothy 5:1-2)*.

Grateful and Positive — Frustrations, adjustments, and relationship disappointments may be many and difficult for the facilitator in a prison ministry. When these setbacks occur, we can remind ourselves that God's will is to be disciplining our attitude toward thankfulness. *Give thanks in all circumstances; for this is the will of God in Christ Jesus for you (1 Thessalonians 5:18).* One does not have to be a Pollyanna, but certainly the Lord would call us to be focusing on His work and ways. In a challenging ministry, it becomes obvious that the Lord is the one who is doing any effective transformation.

Submissive to Authority — From time to time those in charge may seem to be arbitrary or fickle. It is in those occasions we should remind ourselves that respecting authority is not just a safety concern, but also a part of our witness: *Keep your conduct among the Gentiles honorable, so that when they speak against you as evildoers, they may see your good deeds and glorify God on the day of visitation. Be subject for the Lord's sake to every human institution, whether it be to the emperor as supreme, or to governors as sent by him to punish those who do evil and to praise those who do good. For this is the will of God, that by doing good you should put to silence the ignorance of foolish people (1 Peter 2:12-15).*

Access for a Bible study was becoming difficult, and the prison warden was giving hints of its denial. But then a group of prisoners from the study stopped an uprising in the jail. They did this by standing together as Christian brothers across racial lines. It was such an impressive attitude statement. The prison officials subsequently supported and expanded the permission for the ministry.

Evangelical – believing the gospel
Evangelistic – sharing the gospel

Evangelistic — Evangel is the root word for evangelical/evangelistic and can be translated "message, gospel, good tidings." A good number of people may be evangelical (*believing* the gospel); but they are not evangelistic (*sharing* the message). We believe that God wants the gospel to be known by those who have not yet believed. *The Lord is not slow to fulfill His promise as some count slowness,*

CHAPTER 5: GUIDE FOR LIFE CHANGE

but is patient toward you, not wishing that any should perish, but that all should reach repentance (2 Peter 3:9).

Evangelistic in This Ministry

If we are going to have an effective, life-change-involved ministry, we need to have evangelism on our hearts and lips.

Know the gospel for yourself — Perhaps this could go without saying, yet the level of experiential knowledge of the gospel is important. A child is able to believe in Christ and His work for salvation. Growing in faith, love, and hope is a part of the gospel's fruit. Sharing with another so that they put their faith in Christ is a great joy. We want to live out truth on all these levels.

Know how to proclaim and persuade — Chapter 4 was designed to highlight this principle. A proper, recent exhortation to engage in ministry to the poor, oppressed, and imprisoned has given rise to some positive response among church leaders and members. Richard Stearns, President of World Vision®, U. S., recounted how as a young man he had a limited view of the gospel and its impact: "It was about saving as many people from hell as possible — for the next life. It minimized any concern for those same people in this life."[5] Later in his book, *The Hole in Our Gospel*, he outlines three important principles that apply to the ministry to the incarcerated:

1. Every one of these hurting people (naked, a stranger, those in prison) is created in God's image and loved by Him.

2. Every one of these challenges (in ministering to the disadvantaged) has a solution.

3. Every one of us can make a difference.[6]

Interaction for This Ministry

Pray for the ministry — *All* and *every* ministry needs to be saturated in prayer. Speaking of the command in Hebrews 13:3, Gerard Crispin stated, "I am struggling to remember when I last heard anybody pray for prisoners, while having practical compassion on them seems to have few takers."[7] We need the prayer support of our church, our families and friends, and of our own personal times with the Lord. "To pray is to align our desires, passions, and dreams with God's, and that always leads to change, whether dramatic or incremental. Prayer puts us in touch with God's heart, and when prayer is grounded in humility it exposes us to God's priority for the poor and oppressed."[8]

Let it not be said of us who serve in the Lifeline ministry that we do not pray!

Love the people! — They can grow and change! Jesus had compassion on the people of His day, even those who rejected His ministry! *"O Jerusalem, Jerusalem, the city that kills the prophets and stones those who are sent to it! How often would I have gathered your children together as a hen gathers her brood under her wings, and you were not willing!" (Matthew 23:37).*

As a student, a young man who had been discharged from the military but felt the call to ministry began attending college. Many looked at his gruff exterior, brusque manner, and direct speech and thus discounted his fitness for ministry. Happily, a few friends and teachers believed he could move toward roles of service for Christ. In the same way, we need to envision that God can (and does!) reach inmates where they are. He then changes them from the inside out and often places them in a significant role of leadership.

Evaluate judgment — Criticism is difficult to handle, whether deserved or not. When a leader has an attitude of condescension or judgment, the inmates will feel it. "The suggestion I would make to volunteers is to be sensitive about how you are looking at inmates.

They are able to recognize the difference between genuine concern and fascinated curiosity in your eyes."[9]

Prisoners need to know of the total forgiveness through the atonement of Christ, regardless of their past. The Church must also show them how their past can be utilized for God's glory. "Their past sins and present forgiveness, combined with the trials of incarceration, enable them to show compassion toward others — a compassion that begins in prison and accomplishes God's will through a developing priesthood."[10] How do we know we have correct discernment? Inmates are extending proper compassion.

Overcome fear — Fear has the potential to paralyze ministry. Allowing the Lord to overcome that fear through love is essential. *There is no fear in love, but perfect love casts out fear. For fear has to do with punishment, and whoever fears has not been perfected in love. We love because He first loved us (1 John 4:18-19).* A pastor friend of ours feels most people believe the opposite of fear is courage, but often it is love.

> Be a guide by the side, not a sage on the stage!

Be a guide by the side, not a sage on the stage! — This popular phrase has become almost a byword on college campuses. Students either bemoan or laud the professor who fills their files (minds?) with notes. We discussed this training manual with a member of our church. He has considerable prison ministry experience. We determined a spectrum of perspectives on the role of the volunteer guide. They mirror the polar extremes we encounter on college campuses.

On one side of the spectrum is the teacher-directed ministry. Here the teacher does most of the talking. It is the responsibility of the student to listen, perhaps take notes, and at appropriate times ask a question. The dangers of this model of ministry are the student can easily disengage and the instructor will find him or herself talking into thin air.

On the other extreme is the student-led model. Here the students are doing the talking. The teacher is more of a chaperone, refereeing when there is a need for direction or calling a foul, but not actively participating. One of the main dangers of this ministry setting is one of a pooling of ignorance.

Student-centered, teacher-guided

Somewhere in between these two poles is the avenue of greater effectiveness. The student-centered, teacher-guided model allows teacher and students to interact with flexibility and meaning. The teacher's responsibility is to guide, facilitate, and prompt the students to dig into the Word and the curriculum and seek life application. The students know the small group will be safe and formed around meeting their needs — whether they are aware of them or not. This is the preferred way of being a facilitator within the Awana Lifeline ministry. The needs of the students are central, but the guidance comes from a wise and skilled teacher. When a teacher is a facilitator/coach and not a lecturer/preacher the criticism is often made, "They (the students) won't learn as much!" But learning specialists affirm students can learn as much through interaction as they can through lecture. An additional benefit is the communication is greatly superior in changing attitudes.

Know when to teach, when to warn — (Colossians 1:28). Knowing when to admonish and when to let an issue go is a valuable discernment. We trust the Holy Spirit to give us this kind of wisdom (1 John 4:1-3). At times we should withhold teaching also: when we know we are in the presence of a scoffer (Proverbs 9:7-8) or if the student cannot bear any more instruction (John 16:12). Guidance from the Lord, learning from other experienced leaders, and occasional adjustments because of mistakes should be expected.

Handling the Bible Accurately

One would expect an Awana ministry to have the Scriptures in a high and honorable place! Chapter 2 outlined the Bible's priority. When working with inmates, we should guide them into discovery of:

Basics — Using the Bible in Study, Counsel, and Teaching

Inmates may not be familiar with the Scriptures and we will need to teach them the basics. Knowing how to find a reference, a general understanding of the different types of writing in the Bible, and effective uses of the table of contents, concordance, and other Bible helps are essential skills.

A small-group member did not participate during the study, but was fully animated in the conversation after. When asked about any hindrances, he said he was unable to follow where the others found all their information and suggested we use page numbers. After explaining that differing publications of the Bible might make page numbers difficult to use, he gained some experience in searching the references for himself. His participation greatly improved.

Hermeneutics — Understand the Bible by Interpreting It Correctly

Chapter 2 outlined seven principles of handling the Scriptures well in interpretation. Hermeneutics is the science and art of interpreting the Scriptures. The Bible encourages us to be diligent in handling the Scriptures (2 Timothy 2:15) and teachers to be doubly careful in their teaching (James 3:1).

What do you look for as you begin to gain experience in interpreting the Bible? Learning to see is the advice given by Bible theologians Duvall and Hays.[11] A progression of words, sentences, paragraphs and entire books should be followed.

Let the Bible speak and change lives, but be very cautious about getting stalled in questionable practices or endless discussions. In being a good leader, the direct question of "How does the Bible read to you?" will encourage the flow of your discussion.

Understand the Culture of Prison

Chapter 3 gives much information on understanding the incarcerated person. It may be emphasized here, however, that the skills of discerning the needs of an inmate should be pursued. You can learn how to learn about prisoners. Building relationships and asking questions are the keys to knowing and caring about an inmate's life. Some may have a quick and easy rapport. But all of us can develop our observation skills and abilities to respond.

> You can learn how to learn.

METHOD: SMALL-GROUP DYNAMICS

Small-Group Leadership

The most important aspect of the small-group ministry in the jails and prisons is the mindset of the leader. What he or she does is a response to who he or she is! But once the proper motivation is set, how does a leader lead?

Relationship for Connection — Love is the basis for effectiveness in small-group leadership. "You will never earn the right to fully lead those whom you do not love."[12] The leader must model faith, hope, and love as hallmarks of a growing Christian (1 Thessalonians 1). When relationship is established, the connections and dynamics of group process begin to have deeper effect.

> Ministry is best done in the context of relationship.

How does one establish a relationship? Many of the skills already discussed in this book are practical steps in starting and sustaining relationships. Listening to another's story, asking questions to draw closer to the Lord and to each other, conversations that are guided to go deeper, and mutually sharing faith and the gospel are all a part of the small-group leader's set of skills. Ministry is best done in the context of relationship.

As a guide begins his or her small-group experience, communication regarding concerns and joys should be part of the plan. It's not just preliminaries until you can start the study. The sharing, prayer, care, and shepherding a leader does are vital functions of the ministry. The facilitator is not seeking to reach only the cognitive (head), he or she is also setting an environment for life change. That environment is relationally driven. Small-group expert Steve Gladden states one of the key qualities of an effective leader: "Your leaders must have the heart of a shepherd and see each person in their small group as someone within their sphere of influence and care. John 10:1-18 gives us a perfect description of authentic leadership."[13]

If possible, time should be planned for catching up with one another. Philippians 2:1-4 may be the key set of verses as burdens are conveyed and carried together. Prayer and counsel should also be included. A guideline we recommend for small-group leaders is to spend at least one sixth of the allotted time together in sharing and prayer, but not more than one fourth. (This does not include the application-oriented prayer time you may want at the end of your study together.) "Sharing may take place at many different points within the group meetings. It can precede prayer, be a part of discussions focusing on applicational issues, be prompted by life-related Bible study, or be a part of casual conversations before or after the meetings."[14] The leader will have to gauge this carefully, not wanting other purposes to be pinched for time.

Questions for Launching — One of the best ways to get started in small group leadership is … to start! Asking a great question prompts people's thinking. When a person engages in thinking, a person is ready to discuss. Chapter 2 described the launch-connect-understand-connect-apply-close sequence of questions. "A good *launching* question is one that simply asks the group members what they have discovered on their own in a particular section or question in their Bible study preparation."[15] This cycle works effectively for the overall study, but the question-discussion-summary process also is sound facilitation for sharing and prayer. The Navigators suggest three criteria for good questions: "Good questions are clear. Good questions are relevant. Good questions stimulate discussion."[16]

> Good questions are clear. Good questions are relevant. Good questions stimulate discussion.

Discussion About the Bible and Needs of the Inmate — The interchange of tackling the material and seeking application is essential if we are going to be prompting life change. "Planning in opportunities for talking about meanings and experiencing of truth, voicing fears, and sharing questions with one another prepares the ground for new formation to occur."[17]

Keeping on Topic — A discussion plan is usually the best help in keeping a group on topic! This is a difficult balance. On the one hand, the needs of the students were in view when the materials were prayerfully selected and prepared. Alternatively, inmate issues will surface that you will be prompted to address immediately. Experienced leaders seem to be able to handle these brief, side conversations and can get back on track quickly. Sometimes it is appropriate to designate a more suitable time to focus on a particular need of one or two group members.

> Be prepared and passionate but don't preach.

Not Preaching, but Passion — Small-group dynamics are rarely helped when someone begins to preach. We want to be prepared and passionate, but not take over the discussion. Christian educator Harley Atkinson summarizes this important role: "It must be re-emphasized that in a group discussion, the role of the leader is not so much didactic teacher as facilitator. Webster's Collegiate Dictionary defines the word *facilitate* as 'to make easier.' Consequently the task for a small-group Christian education leader or facilitator is to make it easier for small-group members to engage in dialogue or discussion."[18]

Small-Group Skills

Setting a Small-Group Environment — Student-centered, leader-guided small groups are the style of groups we are seeking to establish. To do this, usually groups of five to seven members are optimal. Three attendees in a group are typically the minimum for comfort (except for personal communication times). If a group becomes more than nine, participants usually feel intimidated in sharing and not enough time is given in your study sessions to hear each one.

Confidentiality should be maintained, but be alert: no promises should be made which jeopardize the safety of the inmate or another person. Security procedures need to be strictly followed. Prison chaplains and ministry coordinators will be able to assist you in knowing how to handle difficult issues of concern.

When a Participant Cannot Read — Using Oral Methods — Each chapter of this book provides specific techniques to benefit the group leader when they have a small-group member who cannot read (or struggles to do so). Using story, questions, conversation, pictures, and Scripture memory are oral methods making a group experience much stronger for the nonreader.

Guide Toward Spiritual Discussion and Decision — The priority is for each participant to have an opportunity in responding to the gospel and for growth. Keep a balance between knowledge that is challenging, sharing that leads to accountability, and planning that puts intentions into action.

The tone for active learning is usually set before even beginning, therefore, extra preparation and prayer should precede the first small-group get-together. "Small-group research shows that awareness of belonging, of feeling 'at home,' and of being excited at the possibilities in a small group are frequently connected to active involvement in the first meeting."[19]

Handling Difficult Situations of Participants — Leaders who work closely with others in prison ministry find camaraderie in overcoming many obstacles. If possible, every small-group guide should have an apprentice who is being prepared for the cycle of discipleship via small-group ministry. Also, the mentoring you can receive from other leaders is invaluable.

However, several specific issues arise which will be addressed here. We will look to small-group experts to help us gain their expertise in answering the questions: "How do I deal with a participant who is …?"

1. Reluctant — Hesitant to share

- "Facilitate conversation; value the thoughts and comments of group members.

- The Bible can be a normal part of their lives, model this with your own behavior.

- Share ownership by vision-casting and training of group members; perhaps even sharing leadership responsibilities.

- Spend time together.

- Grow through conflict resolution and ministering to one another."[20]

2. A Talker — Answers every question

- "Position them next to you; this avoids eye contact and if needed, you could reach over and give a slight touch on the arm.

- Whole group talkative? Set a ground rule that says one person talking at a time, with 'taking turns' reinforced with passing around an object or visual cue.

- Look to develop natural leadership abilities — often the case — and discuss how to become a servant guide for the group.
- Problem persists? Get some time alone to talk about giving others a chance to participate."[21]

3. A Non-talker — Does not answer any question. The key may be in developing better questions:

- "Does the question get the group's attention?

- Does it lead to personal involvement?

- Does it leave room for individual creative expression?

- Does it give everyone an opportunity to respond?

- Is it aimed at the group's personal understanding?

- Does it avoid embarrassing any of the group members?

- Don't be afraid of silence, it often is needed for participants to think."[22]

4. A Distractor — Crisis mode, always needy, other problems

- "Care-fronting — combining care and confronting

- Care-fronting — offers genuine caring that bids another grow. To care is to welcome, invite, and support growth in another. It offers real confrontation that calls out new insight and understanding. To confront effectively is to offer the maximum of useful information with the minimum of threat."[23]

Overall Plan for Handling Difficulties
- Recognition — acknowledge the issue/problem; don't hide from it.

- Personalization — understand that problem solving is normal.

- Clarification — identify the problem and seek solutions together.

- Resolution — cooperate (if possible) in dealing with the issue.[24]

ORAL METHOD: SCRIPTURE MEMORY

"Building on its Jewish heritage where the Scriptures were read every week in the synagogue, the early church placed a premium on knowing and memorizing the Scriptures."[25] The ministry in the prison should follow this important trend.

Some criticize Scripture memory as being susceptible to the dangers of being too tied to a schooling performance model and not involved in the complexity of spiritual formation.[26] We suppose that these could be dangers, but we also know the Bible commends putting the Word of God into the heart (Deuteronomy 6:6). *I have stored up Your word in my heart, that I might not sin against You (Psalm 119:11). Your words were found, and I ate them, and Your words became to me a joy and the delight of my heart, for I am called by Your name, O LORD, God of hosts (Jeremiah 15:16).*

A good question to ask is, "How can someone memorize Scripture when he or she cannot read?" By repetition, hearing over and over again the words from the Bible, a person can memorize key verses. Group support is a strong accountability for memorizing Scripture. Singing Scripture (indeed, some Bible books were originally musical!) is also an important method of learning to put Scripture to memory.

TEACHING POINTERS

Teach with music. Too often singing and playing music has been regarded as only for use in worship. But songs have the potential to be educational and prompt or promote fellowship. Music can counsel and assist in Bible memory. One of the first evidences of being filled with the Spirit is a*ddressing one another in psalms and hymns and spiritual songs, singing and making melody to the Lord with your heart (Ephesians 5:19).*

Teach for endurance. "Stay as long as you can!" This is the advice we often give to novice ministers. A normal amount of transition and turnover should be expected in any ministry. However, when little consistency is evident, frustration and missed relationships often occur. While every involvement is appreciated, long-term group facilitators describe greater effectiveness in the ministry as leaders persist and group members are regular in attendance.

Stay as long as you can!

Teach for communication. Healthy small groups have much conversation. In fact, many leaders have difficulty keeping conversation focused. Ralph Neighbor suggests four channels of communication a healthy small group exhibits:

1. God to group. People want to hear from God …

2. Group to God. We not only hear from God, we respond to Him. A response can take the form of a prayer, a praise, a reading of Scripture back to God, a song, or a quiet devotion that expresses feelings to God.

3. Group member to group member. Vulnerable, authentic, truthful communication among group members will enable your group to become a powerful vehicle for life change …

4. Group to the world. It is our responsibility as believers to take the message of Christianity to a lost and dying world.[27]

Notes

1 Lane T. Dennis, executive ed.,"Study Notes on Colossians 1:27-29," *The English Standard Version Study Bible* (Wheaton, IL: Crossway, 2008), p. 2295.

2 A. T. Robertson, *Word Pictures in the New Testament* (Nashville, TN: Broadman Press, 1931), Vol. IV, p. 485.

3 Kenneth S. Wuest, "Ephesians and Colossians in the Greek New Testament," *Wuest's Word Studies From the Greek New Testament* (Grand Rapids, MI: Wm. B. Eerdmans Publishing Company, 1953), p. 194.

4 Lennie Spitale, *Prison Ministry: Understanding Prison Culture Inside and Out* (Nashville, TN: B & H Publishing Group, 2002), p. 21.

5 Richard Stearns, *The Hole in Our Gospel* (Nashville, TN: Thomas Nelson Publishers, 2009), p. 17.

6 Ibid, p. 151.

7 Gerard Crispin, *Beyond Bars: Looking Inside the Inside Story* (Ryelands Road, Leominster, UK: Day One Publications, 2007), p. 8.

8 David W. Crocker, *The Samaritan Way: Lifestyle Compassion Ministry* (St. Louis: Chalice Press, 2008), p. 129.

9 Spitale, *Prison Ministry: Understanding Prison Culture Inside and Out*, p. 98.

10 Henry G. Covert, *Ministry to the Incarcerated* (La Vergne, TN: Henry G. Covert, publisher, 2014), p. 10.

11 J. Scott Duvall and J. Daniel Hays, *Grasping God's Word: A Hands-On Approach to Reading, Interpreting, and Applying the Bible* (Grand Rapids, MI: Zondervan, 2012), p. 69.

12 Bill Donahue, *Leading Life-Changing Small Groups* (Grand Rapids, MI: Zondervan, 2002), p. 38.

13 Steve Gladen, *Small Groups with Purpose: How to Create Healthy Communities* (Grand Rapids. MI: Baker Books, 2011), p. 156.

14 Neal F. McBride, *How to Lead Small Groups* (Colorado Springs: NavPress, 1990), p. 94.

15 The Navigators, *How to Lead Small Group Bible Studies* (Colorado Springs: NavPress, 1982), p. 19.

16 The Navigators, *Lead Out: A Guide for Leading Bible Discussion Groups* (Colorado Springs: NavPress, 1974), p. 22.

17 Julie A. Gorman, *Community That Is Christian: A Handbook on Small Groups* (Grand Rapids, MI: Baker Books, 2002), p. 98.

18 Harley Atkinson, *The Power of Small Groups in Christian Education* (Nappanee, IN: Evangel Publishing House, 2002), p. 274.

19 Julie A. Gorman, "Group Discussion," in Jonathan N. Thigpen, *Teaching Techniques* (Wheaton, IL: Evangelical Training Association, 2001), p. 68.

20 Gladen, *Small Groups with Purpose: How to Create Healthy Communities*, pp. 54-65.

21 Laurie Polich, *The Youth Worker's Pocket Guide to Leading a Small Group* (El Cajon, CA: Youth Specialties, 1997), pp. 28-29.

22 The Navigators, *How to Lead Small Group Bible Studies*, pp. 34, 47.

23 Donahue, *Leading Life-Changing Small Groups*, p. 126.

24 Neal F. McBride, *How to Lead Small Groups*, pp. 105-106.

25 J. Scott Duvall and J. Daniel Hays, *Living God's Word: Discovering Our Place in the Great Story of Scripture* (Grand Rapids, MI: Zondervan, 2012), p. 10.

26 Merilyn J. MacLeod, "Scripture Memory," in *Evangelical Dictionary of Christian Education*, edited by Michael J. Anthony (Grand Rapids, MI: Baker Academic, 2001), p. 619.

27 As summarized by Donahue, *Leading Life-Changing Small Groups*, pp. 85-86.

THE GOSPEL WHEEL

Remember the main thing? It is the gospel.

First, the gospel message comes directly from Scripture. Scripture is the Word of God and His Word is the source on which we rest our faith.

Second, people learn through repetition. Therefore, know the gospel and present it frequently.

The simplicity of the gospel is beautiful. The Gospel Wheel was designed to be a usable tool for presenting the gospel to the post-modern person. You don't have to use an outline, although it is certainly there. Just begin to share with a person from the Scriptures starting at any entry point, and allow the Holy Spirit to use God's Work to lead a person to faith in Christ. Let the Bible speak!

Memorizing these eight verses gives you the ready ability to share the gospel at any time. Also, this diagram will help you be free from a method or script. It allows for both rock-solid truth and flexibility. Sometimes you will share the gospel from one angle and sometimes another. The gospel doesn't change but how we communicate it may. You may also want to use additional verses in your conversations or presentations but these are some foundational verses.

At the center, of course, is the **gospel** (I Corinthians 15:3-4). This is what we believe — that Jesus died for our sins, was buried and rose according to the Scriptures.

The outer circle is partitioned into four segments. The entry points align themselves along two dimensions. The **character** line could begin with a discussion of God's character (loving and holy — John 3:16, Revelation 4:8b), or man's character (sinful — Romans 3:23, Romans 6:23).

Or begin along the **action** axis, where God acts in the cross (Christ's shed blood on the cross provides for our salvation — Romans 5:8), or the corresponding and necessary action of a person, which is to believe (trust — Acts 16:31). Any entry point gets you to the gospel.

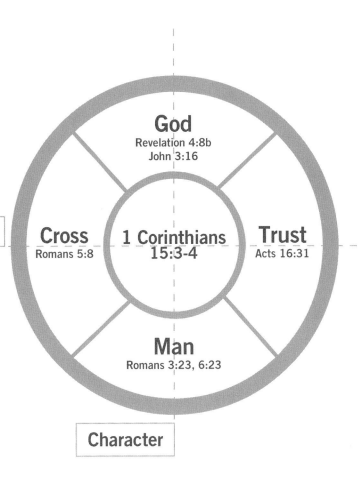

Scripture Memory

Chapter 1: Ministry for Life Change

BIG IDEA

Prison ministry is service to the Lord by visiting, teaching, guiding, and advising those in prison to trust in Christ and to reach out to impact others, especially their children. **Why should I do this?** is the motivational question.

KEY VERSE

Remember the Prisoner — *Remember those who are in prison, as though in prison with them, and those who are mistreated, since you also are in the body. (Hebrews 13:3)*

CHALLENGE VERSE 1

Praying for Prisoners — *So Peter was kept in prison, but earnest prayer for him was made to God by the church. (Acts 12:5)*

CHALLENGE VERSES 2

The Way of the Righteous — *Blessed is the man who walks not in the counsel of the wicked, nor stands in the way of sinners, nor sits in the seat of scoffers; but his delight is in the law of the LORD, and on His law he meditates day and night. He is like a tree planted by streams of water that yields its fruit in its season, and its leaf does not wither. In all that he does, he prospers. The wicked are not so, but are like chaff that the wind drives away. Therefore the wicked will not stand in the judgment, nor sinners in the congregation of the righteous; for the LORD knows the way of the righteous, but the way of the wicked will perish. (Psalm 1)*

Scripture Memory

Chapter 2: Hand on the Word

BIG IDEA

The Word of God is the agent of change in people's lives. Consistent, meaningful study and obedience to the Scriptures is the basis of life change — faith in Christ and growth in Christ. **How do you read it?** is the essential question.

KEY VERSES

Scripture Equips — *All Scripture is breathed out by God and profitable for teaching, for reproof, for correction, and for training in righteousness, that the man of God may be complete, equipped for every good work. (2 Timothy 3:16-17)*

CHALLENGE VERSES 1

Jesus Fulfills Scripture — *The Spirit of the Lord is upon Me, because He has anointed Me to proclaim good news to the poor. He has sent Me to proclaim liberty to the captives and recovering of sight to the blind, to set at liberty those who are oppressed … And He began to say to them, "Today this scripture has been fulfilled in your hearing." (Luke 4:18, 21)*

CHALLENGE VERSES 2

Interpreting Scripture — *And behold, a lawyer stood up to put Him to the test, saying, "Teacher, what shall I do to inherit eternal life?" He said to him, "What is written in the Law? How do you read it?" (Luke 10:25-26)*

Scripture Memory

Chapter 3: Hand on the Student

BIG IDEA

Building a relationship with the people in your sphere of influence (small group) to guide and facilitate faith and spiritual growth is the environment for life change, both in the inmates' lives and in those of their families. **What does this person need?** is the relational question.

KEY VERSES

Minister to the Least of These — *And when did we see You sick or in prison and visit You? And the King will answer them, "Truly, I say to you, as you did it to one of the least of these My brothers, you did it to Me." (Matthew 25:39-40)*

CHALLENGE VERSE 1

Heart in View — *For the LORD sees not as man sees: man looks on the outward appearance, but the LORD looks on the heart. (1 Samuel 16:7b)*

CHALLENGE VERSES 2

Encouragement in Christ — *So if there is any encouragement in Christ, any comfort from love, any participation in the Spirit, any affection and sympathy, complete my joy by being of the same mind, having the same love, being in full accord and of one mind. Do nothing from selfish ambition or conceit, but in humility count others more significant than yourselves. Let each of you look not only to his own interests, but also to the interests of others. (Philippians 2:1-4)*

Scripture Memory

Chapter 4: Gospel of Grace

BIG IDEA

The gospel of grace is the power of God to change a person's life. Clearly and confidently sharing the message of truth is the joy and witness of the facilitator in prison ministry. **What must I do to be saved?** is the salvation question.

KEY VERSES

Invitation to a Prison Guard — *Then he brought them out and said, "Sirs, what must I do to be saved?" And they said, "Believe in the Lord Jesus, and you will be saved, you and your house-hold." (Acts 16:30-31)*

CHALLENGE VERSES 1

Summary of the Gospel — *For I delivered to you as of first importance what I also received: that Christ died for our sins in accordance with the Scriptures, that He was buried, that He was raised on the third day in accordance with the Scriptures, and that He appeared to Cephas, then to the twelve. (1 Corinthians 15:3-5)*

CHALLENGE VERSE 2

Power of the Gospel — *For I am not ashamed of the gospel, for it is the power of God for salvation to everyone who believes, to the Jew first and also to the Greek. (Romans 1:16)*

Scripture Memory

Chapter 5: Guide for Life Change

BIG IDEA

Being prepared for prison ministry in knowledge, attitude, and skills is the goal of the servant of Christ. Serving the Lord and leading those entrusted to my care fulfills the call to ministry. **How do I do this?** is the operational question.

KEY VERSES

Ministry of Maturity/Christlikeness — *Him we proclaim, warning everyone and teaching everyone with all wisdom, that we may present everyone mature in Christ. For this I toil, struggling with all His energy that He powerfully works within me. (Colossians 1:28-29)*

CHALLENGE VERSES 1

Paul's Testimony — *And now, behold, I am going to Jerusalem, constrained by the Spirit, not knowing what will happen to me there, except that the Holy Spirit testifies to me in every city that imprisonment and afflictions await me. But I do not account my life of any value nor as precious to myself, if only I may finish my course and the ministry that I received from the Lord Jesus, to testify to the gospel of the grace of God. (Acts 20:22-24)*

CHALLENGE VERSES 2

Exhortations for Leaders — *And we urge you, brothers, admonish the idle, encourage the fainthearted, help the weak, be patient with them all. See that no one repays anyone evil for evil, but always seek to do good to one another and to everyone. Rejoice always, pray without ceasing. (1 Thessalonians 5:14-17)*

Aitken, Jonathan. *Charles W. Colson: A Life Redeemed*. Colorado Springs: Waterbrook Press, 2005.

Andrews, Reddit III. "Sin and the Fall," in *The Gospel as Center: Renewing Our Faith and Reforming Our Ministry Practices*, edited by Timothy Keller and D. A. Carson. Wheaton, IL: The Gospel Coalition, Crossway, 2012.

Arch, Dave. *Creative Training Techniques*. Minneapolis: The Bob Pike Group, 2000.

Atkinson, Harley. *The Power of Small Groups in Christian Education*. Nappanee, IN: Evangel Publishing House, 2002.

Awana Clubs International website at awana.org, 2014.

Awana Lifeline website at awanalifeline.org, 2014.

Awana Lifeline. *Malachi Dads: The Heart of a Father*. Streamwood, IL: Awana Clubs International, 2013.

Beckwith, Ivy. *Formational Children's Ministry: Shaping Children Using Story, Ritual, and Relationship*. Grand Rapids, MI: Baker Books, 2010.

Benson, Clarence, *Biblical Beliefs: Doctrines Believers Should Know*. Wheaton, IL: Evangelical Training Association, 2001.

Bird, Michael S. *Evangelical Theology*. Grand Rapids, MI: Zondervan, 2013.

Bounds, E. M. *The Complete Works of E. M. Bounds on Prayer*. Grand Rapids, MI: Baker Book House, 1990.

Braman, Donald. *Doing Time on the Outside: Incarceration and Family Life in Urban America*. Ann Arbor: University of Michigan Press, 2009.

Brother Lawrence. *The Practice of the Presence of God*. San Francisco: Riven Press Classics, 2013.

Cahill, Mark. *One Thing You Can't Do in Heaven*. Rockwall, TX: Biblical Discipleship Ministries, 2004.

Carlson, Gregory C. "Preparing Yourself in the Word," *Understanding Teaching*. Wheaton, IL: Evangelical Training Association, Instructional Resource Guide, Worksheets 9 & 10, 1998.

Carlson, Gregory C. *Rock Solid Teacher: Discover the Joy of Teaching Like Jesus*. Ventura, CA: Gospel Light, 2006.

Carlson, Jason. "Jesus: Risen for a New Generation," in *Apologetics for a New Generation*, general editor Sean McDowell. Eugene, OR: Harvest House Publishers, 2009. (V

Carson, D. A. and Timothy Keller. "Gospel Centered Ministry" in *The Gospel as Center: Renewing Our Faith and Reforming Our Ministry Practices*, edited by Timothy Keller and D. A. Carson. Wheaton, IL: The Gospel Coalition, Crossway. 2012.

Chan, Francis. *Crazy Love: Overwhelmed by a Relentless God*. Colorado Springs: David C. Cook, 2008.

Chapell, Bryan. "What is the Gospel?" in *The Gospel as Center: Renewing Our Faith and Reforming Our Ministry Practices*, edited by Timothy Keller and D. A. Carson. Wheaton, IL: The Gospel Coalition, Crossway, 2012.

Covert, Henry G. *Ministry to the Incarcerated*. Chicago: Loyola Press, 1995.

Covert, Henry G. *Ministry to the Incarcerated*. La Vergne, TN: Henry G. Covert publisher, 2014 (updated edition).

Crispin, Gerard. *Beyond Bars: Looking Inside the Inside Story*. Ryelands Road, Leominster, UK: Day One Publications, 2007.

Crocker, David W. *The Samaritan Way: Lifestyle Compassion Ministry*. St. Louis: Chalice Press, 2008.

Dennis, Lane T., executive ed. "Introduction to Proverbs," *ESV Study Bible, English Standard Version*. Wheaton, IL: Crossway, 2008.

Dennis, Lane T., executive ed. "Study Notes on Colossians 1:27-29," *The English Standard Version Study Bible*. Wheaton, IL: Crossway, 2008.

Dennis, Lane T., executive ed. "The Bible and Revelation," *ESV Study Bible, English Standard Version*. Wheaton, IL: Crossway, 2008.

Detzler, Wayne A. *New Testament Words in Today's Language*. Wheaton, IL: Victor Books, 1986.

Dolan, Kelly. In Michael Novelli, *Shaped by the Story: Discover the Art of Bible Storytelling*. Minneapolis: Spark House, 2013.

BIBLIOGRAPHY

Donahue, Bill. *Leading Life-Changing Small Groups*. Grand Rapids, MI: Zondervan, 2002.

Dr. Kristi Miller, conversation at Louisiana State Prison for Women, February 6, 2014.

Duvall, J. Scott and J. Daniel Hays. *Grasping God's Word: A Hands-on Approach to Reading, Interpreting, and Applying the Bible*. Grand Rapids, MI: Zondervan, 2012.

Duvall, J. Scott and J. Daniel Hays. *Living God's Word: Discovering Our Place in the Great Story of Scripture*. Grand Rapids, MI: Zondervan, 2012.

Eggen, Paul D. and Donald P. Kauchak. Referencing McKeachie and Kulik in *Strategies for Teachers: Teaching Content and Thinking Skills*. Boston: Allyn and Bacon, 1996.

Fay, William and Ralph Hodge. *Share Jesus Without Fear*. Nashville, TN: LifeWay Press, 1997.

Gladen, Steve. *Small Groups with Purpose: How to Create Healthy Communities*. Grand Rapids. MI: Baker Books, 2011.

Glaze, Lauren E. and Erinn J. Herberman. "Correctional Populations in the United States, 2012," *Bureau of Justice Statistics Bulletin*, www.ojp.usdoj.gov. U.S. Department of Justice, Office of Justice Programs, December 2013.

Godawa, Brian. "Storytelling and Persuasion," in *Apologetics for a New Generation*, general editor Sean McDowell. Eugene, OR: Harvest House Publishers, 2009.

Gorman, Julie A. *Community That Is Christian: A Handbook on Small Groups*, 2nd edition. Grand Rapids, MI: Baker Books, 2002.

Gorman, Julie A. "Group Discussion," in Jonathan N. Thigpen, *Teaching Techniques*. Wheaton, IL: Evangelical Training Association, 2001.

Gospel Light. *How to Teach Kids Using Guided Conversation (Grades 1-6)*. Ventura, CA: Gospel Light, 1993.

Hendricks, Howard. *Living By the Book*. Chicago: Moody Press, 1991.

BIBLIOGRAPHY

Horner, Grant. *Meaning at the Movies: Becoming a Discerning Viewer.* Wheaton, IL: Crossway, 2010.

Jones, Timothy Paul. *Family Ministry Field Guide: How Your Church Can Equip Parents to Make Disciples.* Indianapolis: Wesleyan Press, 2011.

Keller, Timothy. *Center Church: Doing Balanced, Gospel-Centered Ministry in Your City.* Grand Rapids, MI: Zondervan, 2012.

Keller, W. Phillip. *A Shepherd Looks at Psalm 23.* Grand Rapids, MI: Zondervan, 1997.

Kennedy, D. James. *Evangelism Explosion.* Wheaton, IL: Tyndale House Publishers, 1970, 1983.

Lampman, Lisa Barnes and Michelle D. Shattuck. "Finding God in the Wake of Crime: Answers to Hard Questions," in *God and the Victim: Theological Reflections on Evil, Victimization, Justice and Forgiveness.* Grand Rapids, MI: William B. Eerdmans Publishing Co., 1999.

Lewis, Jacqueline J. *Power of Stories: A Guide for Leading Multi-Racial and Multi-Cultural Congregations.* Nashville, TN: Abingdon Press, 2008.

MacLeod, Merilyn J. "Scripture Memory," in *Evangelical Dictionary of Christian Education*, edited by Michael J. Anthony. Grand Rapids, MI: Baker Academic, 2001.

McBride, Neal F. *How to Lead Small Groups.* Colorado Springs: NavPress, 1990.

Miller, Kristi. *Hannah's Gift: The Heart of a Mother.* Streamwood, IL: Awana Clubs International, 2013.

New Life Corrections Ministry, Wayside Cross Ministries. *Transforming Dads Incarcerated.* Aurora, IL: New Life Corrections Ministry, Wayside Cross Ministries, Tom Beatty, director, n.d.

Newman, Randy. *Bringing the Gospel Home: Witnessing to Family Members, Close Friends, and Others Who Know You Well.* Wheaton, IL: Crossway, 2011.

Newton, Gary. *Heart-Deep Teaching: Engaging Students for Transformed Lives.* Nashville, TN: B & H Publishing, 2012.

Parrett, Gary A. and S. Steve Kang. *Teaching the Faith, Forming the Faithful*. Downers Grove, IL: IVP Academic, 2009.

Perry, John. *God Behind Bars: The Amazing Story of Prison Fellowship*. Nashville, TN: W Publishing Group, 2006.

Phillips, Richard D. "Can We Know the Truth?" in *The Gospel as Center: Renewing Our Faith and Reforming Our Ministry Practices*, edited by Timothy Keller and D. A. Carson. Wheaton, IL: The Gospel Coalition, Crossway, 2012.

Polich, Laurie. *The Youth Worker's Pocket Guide to Leading a Small Group*. El Cajon, CA: Youth Specialties, 1997.

Powell, Kara E., Brad M. Griffin, and Cheryl A. Crawford. *Sticky Faith*. Grand Rapids, MI: Zondervan, 2011.

Radmacher, Earl D. In Jody Dillow, *The Reign of the Servant Kings*. Hayesville, NC: Schoettle Publishing Co., 1992.

Rahn, Dave and Terry Linhart. *Contagious Faith*. Loveland, CO: Group Publishing, 2000.

Returning Hearts is a ministry strategy of Awana Lifeline. It is a celebration where inmates and their children can unite for a day of games, food, relationship building, biblical teaching, and possibly reconciliation. See www.awanalifeline.org/#/programs/returning-hearts.

Richards, Lawrence O. *Expository Dictionary of Bible Words*. Grand Rapids, MI: Zondervan, 1985.

Richards, Lawrence O. *The Teacher's Commentary*. Wheaton, IL: Victor Books, 1987.

Rienow, Rob. *Limited Church: Unlimited Kingdom; Uniting Church and Family in the Great Commission*. Nashville, TN: Randall House, 2013.

Riggs, Kevin. *Evangelism for the 21st Century*. Wheaton, IL: Evangelical Training Association, 2014.

Robertson, A. T. *Word Pictures in the New Testament*, vol. 4. Nashville, TN: Broadman Press, 1931.

Rorheim, Art. *Fathers Again*. Streamwood, IL: Awana Clubs International, 2008.

BIBLIOGRAPHY

Rose Publishing. *What the Bible Says About Forgiveness*. Torrance, CA: Rose Publishing, Inc., 2011.

Schoonmaker, Paul D. *The Prison Connection*. Valley Forge, PA: Judson Press, 1978.

Simpson, Michael L. *Permission Evangelism: When to Talk, When to Walk*. Colorado Springs: Cook Communications Ministries, 2003.

Spitale, Lennie. *Prison Ministry: Understanding Prison Culture Inside and Out*. Nashville, TN: B & H Publishing Group, 2002.

Stearns, Richard. *The Hole in Our Gospel*. Nashville, TN: Thomas Nelson Publishers, 2009.

Stonehouse, Catherine. "Conversation," *Evangelical Dictionary of Christian Education*, edited by Michael J. Anthony. Grand Rapids, MI: Baker Academic, 2001.

Stott, John. *Understanding the Bible*. Grand Rapids, MI: Baker Books, 1984, 2001.

The Gospel Wheel is a visual means of sharing the gospel using Scripture. It is available in Appendix A of this book and online as the Awana Gospel Message App.

The Navigators. *Bridge to Life*. Colorado Springs: NavPress, 2007.

The Navigators. *How to Lead Small Group Bible Studies*. Colorado Springs: NavPress, 1982.

The Navigators. *Lead Out: A Guide for Leading Bible Discussion Groups*. Colorado Springs: NavPress,1974.

Vine, W. E. *An Expository Dictionary of New Testament Words*, vol 2. Old Tappan, NJ: Fleming H. Revell Company, 1940, 1966.

Watts, W. Jackson. *Biblical Beliefs: Doctrines Believers Should Know*. Wheaton, IL: Evangelical Training Association, 2013.

White, Jerry and Mary. *To Be a Friend: Building Deep and Lasting Relationships*. Colorado Springs: NavPress, 2014.

Wilhoit, James C. and Leland Ryken. *Effective Bible Teaching*, 2nd edition. Grand Rapids, MI: Baker Academic, 2012.

BIBLIOGRAPHY

Williams, Marvin L. *Beyond the Bars: The Black Church and Its Responsibility in Prison/Aftercare Ministry.* Unpublished thesis, Trinity Evangelical Divinity School, 1993.

Wuest, Kenneth S. "Ephesians and Colossians in the Greek New Testament," *Wuest's Word Studies From the Greek New Testament.* Grand Rapids, MI: Wm. B. Eerdmans Publishing Company, 1953.

Yount, William R. *The Teaching Ministry of the Church*, 2nd ed. Nashville, TN: B & H Publishing Group, 2008.

Yuan, Angela and Christopher. *Out of a Far Country.* Colorado Springs: WaterBrook Press, 2011.

Zuck, Roy B. *Basic Bible Interpretation.* Colorado Springs: Cook Communications Ministries, 1991.

Also from Awana Lifeline ...

Hannah's Gift: The Heart of a Mother

Modeled after the life of Hannah
and her son as told in the first two
chapters of 1 Samuel in the Old
Testament, this curriculum offers
mothers the opportunity to parent
from a distance and give a legacy
of faith to their children.

Item 95241

Heart of a Mother, Spanish
Item 97684

Hannah's Gift: Family Restoration

From the first Hannah's Gift book,
incarcerated moms have established
the importance of on-going activity in
the lives of their children. Moms must
now take steps to prepare themselves
to build healthy family structures upon
release. We want to use the prophet
Jeremiah's words and warnings as sign-
posts to lead us along the journey to
healthy relationships.

Item 97472

Malachi Dads: The Heart of a Father

The Heart of a Father curriculum provides practical, biblical advice for life, marriage, and parenting, showing participants how to become Christ- followers and grow in their faith. The *Inmate Challenge DVD*, sold separately, is part of the Malachi Dads curriculum, The Hearts of a Father. Make sure you order a copy with your books.

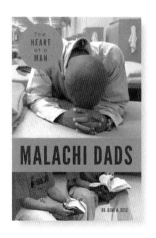

Item 95259

Heart of a Father, Spanish
Item 96935

Malachi Dads: The Heart of a Man, Part 1

The Heart of a Man, Part 1 is the second book in the Malachi Dads' curriculum. This study focuses on how to become a man with a heart that pleases God, no matter what our past sins and failures, and no matter our physical appearance.

Item 97523

Order today!

EMAIL: awanalifeline@awana.org
PHONE: 888-944-4292
ONLINE: awanalifeline.org/products

Also from Awana Lifeline ...

Psalm 1, The Blessed Man

Psalm One is a favorite chapter in the lives of Malachi Dads across the country. This six week study was written by the Malachi Dad inmates at Louisiana State Penitentiary and is now part of the curriculum.

Item 97676

Inmate Challenge DVD

Receive a compelling challenge
from some of the most broken
men in our society — inmate
fathers.

Filmed on location at the famed
Angola Prison in Louisiana,
three inmate fathers share their
stories and their challenge to
other inmates. This DVD is an
ideal launching point for jail or
prison ministry and for challenging fathers to
consider the legacy they are leaving. Includes a five-week
small group discussion guide. Order along with Malachi Dads:
The Heart of a Father curriculum. Running time: 45 minutes.
Includes a five-week small group discussion guide.

Item 83509

Order today!

EMAIL: awanalifeline@awana.org
PHONE: 888-944-4292
ONLINE: awanalifeline.org/products